THE *WETIKO* LEGAL PRINCIPLES

Cree and Anishinabek Responses to Violence and Victimization

In Cree and Anishinabek traditions, the *wetiko* is a cannibal giant or an evil spirit that possesses a person, rendering them monstrous. In *The* Wetiko *Legal Principles*, Hadley Louise Friedland explores how the concept of a *wetiko* can be used to address the unspeakable happenings that endanger the lives of many Indigenous children.

Friedland critically analyses Cree and Anishinabek stories and oral histories alongside current academic and legal literature to find solutions to the frightening rates of intimate violence and child victimization in Indigenous communities. She applies common-law legal analysis to these Indigenous stories and creates a framework for analysing them in terms of the legal principles that they contain. The author reveals similarities in thinking and theorizing about the dynamics of *wetiko*s and offenders in cases of child sexual victimization. Friedland's respectful, strength-based, trauma-informed approach builds on the work of John Borrows and is the first to argue for a legal category derived from Indigenous legal traditions. *The* Wetiko *Legal Principles* provides much-needed direction for effectively applying Indigenous legal principles to contemporary social issues.

HADLEY LOUISE FRIEDLAND is an assistant professor in the Faculty of Law at the University of Alberta. She was the first Research Director of the University of Victoria's Indigenous Law Research Unit.

T0323759

HADLEY LOUISE FRIEDLAND

The *Wetiko* Legal Principles

Cree and Anishinabek Responses to Violence and Victimization

UNIVERSITY OF TORONTO PRESS
Toronto Buffalo London

ISBN 978-1-4875-0256-0 (cloth)
ISBN 978-1-4875-2202-5 (paper)

Library and Archives Canada Cataloguing in Publication

Friedland, Hadley Louise, 1976–, author
The wetiko legal principles : Cree and Anishinabek
responses to violence and victimization / Hadley Louise Friedland.

Includes bibliographical references.
ISBN 978-1-4875-0256-0 (cloth). – ISBN 978-1-4875-2202-5 (paper)

1. Native children – Abuse of – Canada.   2. Native children – Legal
status, laws, etc. – Canada.   3. Child abuse – Law and legislation –
Canada.   4. Native peoples – Canada – Folklore.   5. Legal literature –
Canada.   6. Windigos.   I. Title.

KIB422.F74 2018   362.76089′97071   C2017-906328-6

This book has been published with the help of a grant from the Federation
for the Humanities and Social Sciences, through the Awards to Scholarly
Publications Program, using funds provided by the Social Sciences and
Humanities Research Council of Canada.

University of Toronto Press acknowledges the financial assistance to its
publishing program of the Canada Council for the Arts and the Ontario
Arts Council, an agency of the Government of Ontario.

This book is dedicated to Nina Louise, whom I knew as a fiercely intelligent, inquisitive, and irrepressible thirteen-year-old, and who is now beyond all harm. And to Peacha, who taught me so much about courage, compassion, and perseverance.

. . . what if no lost child can be replaced?

– Emil Fackenheim

Contents

Foreword

Professor Hadley Louise Friedland is one of the most innovative scholars working with Indigenous legal traditions in the world today. Her writing and teaching is nuanced and accessible. It is theoretically rich and exceptionally practical. Indigenous communities are drawing new insights from their legal inheritance through her work. For example, her affiliation with the University of Victoria's Indigenous Law Research Unit is breaking new ground in revitalizing Indigenous law. Lawyers, law professors, and students are also gaining fresh views as they read and apply her research. I have taught from this book in its manuscript form for many years. Each time it is assigned, students report it is one of the best things they have read in law school. I agree. My own understanding of Cree and Anishinaabe law has been significantly enhanced through reading this work. At the same time my understanding of the common law itself has also grown from studying this book.

The question animating this work is: How do we protect the people we love from the people we love? This is an issue that affects all communities. Violence is most frequently perpetrated by those who live and work in close proximity to one another. Women and children bear the brunt of this abuse. This is a world-wide phenomenon.[1] At the same time Indigenous peoples in North America suffer from higher rates of violence than the general population. Thus, intimate violence must be understood and addressed within an Indigenous framework too. As noted, this book takes up this task in brilliant ways.

---

1 World Health Organization, *Fact Sheet, Violence against Women, Intimate Partner and Sexual Violence against Women*, November 2016, at http://www.who.int/mediacentre/factsheets/fs239/en/.

Indigenous peoples were no strangers to violence prior to European colonization. Our stories make it clear that we have experienced traumatic family violence throughout history.[2] This violence was likewise gendered, and women bore its brunt.[3] Jealousy, pride, anger, resentment, hatred, bitterness, desperation, and hopelessness were part of Indigenous peoples' lives before other peoples arrived on our shores. At the same time Indigenous peoples were also resilient, wise, caring, compassionate, thoughtful, patient, and kind. These conditions led to a rich catalogue of stories chronicling violence and our reactions to it. As such, these stories also demonstrate that we had responses to violence that attempted to prevent, punish, and rehabilitate those who caused these horrors.

Wetiko (or Wiindigok as they are called in Anishinaabemowin) are an example of one type of story which shows Indigenous experiences and responses to violence. As Professor Friedland so skilfully demonstrates in the following pages, wetiko are people who experience great stress and who in turn place considerable pressure on those around them. Not all wetiko are violent, though some are. Not all wetiko are dealt with harshly, though some are, as Indigenous law struggles like other legal systems to effectively deal with violence and the harm it causes to those who perpetrate and receive it. The point made in this book is that Indigenous peoples, through the stories they tell and actions they take, are a law-making people too.

Not all law flows from courts, legislatures, or parliaments. Law was made in varied local settings before nation-state formation. Law is also developed in these locations after state formation too, particularly in Indigenous contexts where state law is ineffective because of its imposed, foreign, authoritarian, or dismissive nature. The failure of state law to be persuasive and credible within Indigenous contexts propels people to turn to their own authorities, standards, measures, precedents, and norms to regulate behaviour and resolve disputes.

---

2 For further exploration of this issue, see Emily Snyder, Val Napoleon, and John Borrows, "Gender and Violence: Drawing on Indigenous Legal Resources" (2015) 48 UBC Law Review 593–654.

3 Indigenous Law Research Unit, Gender inside Indigenous Law Toolkit, University of Victoria, Faculty of Law, at https://www.uvic.ca/law/assets/docs/ilru/Gender%20 Inside%20Indigenous%20Law%20Toolkit%2001.01.16.pdf; Indigenous Law Research Unit, Gender inside Indigenous Law Casebook, at https://www.uvic.ca/law/assets/ docs/ilru/Gender%20Inside%20Indigenous%20Law%20Casebook%2001.01.16.pdf.

The *wetiko* stories in this book are examples of this fact. As Professor Friedland demonstrates, they are intermingled with other sources and forms of law to address pressing legal problems.

Wetiko stories must be interpreted in contemporary contexts to ensure the safety and protection of families and communities is strengthened and enhanced. They must also be applied in ways which understand the gendered, multidisciplinary, and cultured contexts of law. Professor Friedland is careful to show how *wetiko* law is/can be appraised and applied in ways which strengthen protections for all involved in this challenging issue: protecting those we love, from those we love.

Every society is a work in progress; peace building is not a passive activity. Anishinaabe, Cree, and other Indigenous law can be a powerful resource for cultivating justice and social order in its context. This book is at the cutting-edge of its field. I recommend it in the highest terms.

John Borrows
Canada Research Chair in Indigenous Law
University of Victoria Law School

Preface

A pressing contemporary issue within Indigenous communities is the frightening rates of internal violence and child victimization. How do we speak of unspeakable things? How do we protect those we love – *from* those we love? Can we reject monstrous actions without rejecting the actor as a monster? And what resources do we need to think through such terrible things in principled and effective ways? This book explores possible answers to these questions within Cree and Anishinabek legal traditions, as described in *wetiko* (windigo) stories.

Both child victimization and the *wetiko* are unspeakable subjects. Most often unspeakable subjects involve unspeakable suffering. However, at times subjects become unspeakable because they are forced to remain unspoken for such a long time. This is the result of oppressive practices so pervasive, dominant, and prolonged that reason succumbs to fatigue and almost all words are lost. It is no coincidence, in my opinion, that the latter often correlates with an increase in the former. The profound social suffering and inter-generational violence common within colonized and oppressed communities illustrates this again and again, through history and across the globe.

At this point in history, the situation for Indigenous children can look bleak. There are more Indigenous children in care today than there were at the height of the residential school era. Once Indigenous children are in care, they have the highest rates of placement breakdowns, are the most likely to "age out" of the system rather than exiting due to reunification or adoption, and generally have the worst overall outcomes of all children in care. There are tragic cases of suicide and deaths, and for those who survive, a childhood in care too often becomes a terrible "pipeline" to adult incarceration or prostitution. It is little wonder that there are increasing cries for ways to ensure Indigenous children can remain within family, community, and culture. Yet in this generation there are also unprecedented levels of violence and child victimization inside Indigenous communities. Horror stories to rival those of government care emerge from within Indigenous communities as well, from horrific cases of abuse, to suicide epidemics. The urge to despair, or to turn away from such intractable suffering, is almost irresistible. Words fail us.

The *wetiko* (or windigo) concept has existed within Cree and Anishinabek societies for centuries. It has most often been translated into English as "cannibal," but it clearly encompasses more than literal flesh-eating. Beyond the ancient stories of cannibal giants who roamed the land, the concept is used to describe human beings who do monstrous things. The majority of non-Indigenous reactions to and treatment of the *wetiko* concept encapsulates the broader colonial issue of forcible dismissal and denigration of Indigenous capacity and thought. The *wetiko* concept was viewed as a disturbing but fascinating cultural oddity and was a salacious topic of study for anthropologists and psychologists for many years. Most characterized it as either a group superstition or a culturally bound psychosis. Few focused on responses to the *wetiko*.

In the late nineteenth century and early twentieth century, respected Indigenous leaders were put on trial, jailed, and even executed for taking part in the execution of a *wetiko*, even in cases where the *wetiko* was endangering the entire community and did not respond to lesser measures, including extensive attempts at healing and laborious supervision. It did not help when these leaders and other community members testified to their authority, decision-making process, and principled reasoning in detail. Their only defences in the non-Indigenous courts, which never succeeded at any rate, were pleas that they were too childlike, superstitious, or uncivilized to have formed the necessary intent for a conviction. While some non-Indigenous allies intervened on their behalf, attesting to these leaders' crucial roles in the community as well as their reputations and reasoning abilities, these efforts at best mitigated a sentence of death to one of life imprisonment, as the colonial government pushed to assert sovereignty over a vast land. Words failed them.

It is little wonder that a deep silence ensued. Given the demeaning characterizations of the *wetiko* concept, and the brutal, humiliating treatment of those who adhered to it, who would want to or even dare to speak of the concept to outsiders? In the powerlessness, turmoil, and doubt engendered by the executions of respected authorities, who had been relied on to keep peace and order, who would dare act upon related responsibilities inside communities? Imagine today if we heard judges and police officers were being imprisoned and executed for carrying out their duties. I suspect public legal reasoning and law enforcement would become unspeakable quite quickly. The consequent silence and impunity are ideal conditions for abuse, and abusers, to flourish. Extreme uncertainty and inefficiency undermine and erode the legitimacy of any legal principles or practices.

In this book I set out to see how the practical and intellectual resources of the *wetiko* concept, rendered unspeakable for so long, can be recovered and re-examined to address the unspeakable happenings that endanger far too many Indigenous children today. I proceed by first examining the academic and legal literature alongside published Cree and Anishinabek stories and oral histories. From this I conclude the *wetiko* is best understood as a complex legal concept or categorization. I then demonstrate the similar thinking and theorizing around the dynamics of *wetiko*s and offenders in cases of child victimization. Next, I outline the legal principles that emerge from a legal analysis of *wetiko* stories and accounts. Finally, I discuss possible future directions for and barriers to applying these legal principles to contemporary issues of violence and child victimization.

This book is a thought experiment. In it, I engage with Indigenous stories as jurisprudence. I take stories seriously, as a means of expression, as a form of reasoning, and as normative resources. For this reason, I begin and end with an original story, in which I use a *wetiko* as a metaphor to capture the current predicaments of child victimization within Indigenous communities. I also take common-law legal reasoning and analysis seriously. I apply these intellectual tools to create a framework for thinking about the *wetiko* stories in terms of legal principles, which could be applied to contemporary issues today.

Although flowing between narrative and legal analysis may at first seem strange to the reader, in the end, I believe these forms of thinking can complement each other and can be combined to develop new insights and approaches in law. I am aware I am combining things that are not usually combined, and that the conclusions I reach are just possibilities. The effort put into this thought experiment simply asserts that there are identifiably legal resources *within* Indigenous societies. In the fraught and urgent area of violence and child victimization within Indigenous communities, such possibilities are worth exploring. We need to seek out every voice to break the silence. We need to access every possibility if we hope to end the relentless suffering in this generation.

Acknowledgments

Warm and heartfelt thanks to the Cree elders and other knowledge-holders in northern Alberta who participated in interviews for this project, for your openness, advice, and endless patience explaining things to me. I am grateful for the time I had with elder Dean Wanyandie, who first told me stories of *wetiko*s during a walk by a river when I was fifteen, setting me on the path that led to this book. Elder Adelaide McDonald has generously shared her immense knowledge, experience, and insight with me for many years, and continues to do so. You are my greatest teacher, and I am humbled and honoured to share some of your teachings and stories in this book. Carol Wanyandie's clear, principled, and compassionate thinking has had a substantial influence on this project. I still have a lot to learn. All mistakes are my own.

Many thanks to Val Napoleon, who pressed my thinking, shored up my spirit, encouraged my ideas, and fed me soup, often all at once. Your ideas, vision, and strength continue to inspire me. This book would not have been imaginable without the ground-breaking and foundational work of John Borrows. For me and many others, your work opened new worlds by bridging two worlds that often feel achingly far apart. I am humbled and grateful to all those who have shared, taught with, and been willing to learn from the manuscript of this book already. I am also thankful for feedback from two anonymous reviewers, who helped me crystallize my thinking, and for the editing team at the University of Toronto Press, who have been a pleasure to work with.

This book would not be what it is without conversations with friends, colleagues, and mentors, including Elizabeth Adjin-Tettey, Karen Ameyaw, Dana Antaya-Moore, Collette Arcand, Ben Berger, J.D. Crookshanks, Ted DeCoste, Liz Greenaway, Jennifer Haslett, Fiona Kelly, Tim

Kelly, Freya Kodar, Alice Moberly, Brenda Parlee, Tina Pysemany, Kendall Stavast, Joana Thackery, James Tully, and Moin Yahya. I owe a substantial debt to Nathan Carlson, for generously sharing your time and research on the *wetiko* concept. Many thanks to Rebecca Johnson, for showing me how law and emotion co-exist, and for always being there. Thank you to Jeremy Webber, for creating space for these ideas with your own work, for always being willing to discuss and nurture new ideas, and for quietly devoting many hours towards making this project possible. Jodi Stonehouse's insights and encouragement pushed this project forward. Kerry Sloan's thorough reading of the text and valuable suggestions helped develop the final draft, and Jess Friedland's precision and attention to detail refined it.

Finally, a special thank you must go to my mom, Joan Friedland, without whose support this project would not have been possible, my partner, Ken McDonald, for keeping me grounded and never letting me give up or give in to outside pressures, and my children, Davita and Asher, for their patience, wisdom, and occasional heckling. Thanks for ensuring I keep perspective – always.

THE *WETIKO* LEGAL PRINCIPLES

Cree and Anishinabek Responses to
Violence and Victimization

Sweet Dirt

All sorrows can be borne if you can put them into a story.[1]

Up in the mountains there was a small community. Now, for many years, people came and went when they wanted, as they wished. Sometimes the families came together for months, to visit and tell stories, to dance, to laugh and tease each other. Once in a while, one or two might even fall in love. Other times, families would head out trapping, curl up around the fire, walk all day, and fall asleep exhausted at night. In those times, when a visitor came, it lit up the night, and when no one was around, the soft comfort of those you knew well from birth surrounded you like snow on the landscape. Rarely, but memorably, this routine would be broken by the arrival of another family, seeking help and medicines for someone who had fallen ill, or who had become a *wetiko* during the long winter. Sometimes, someone would know the right medicine and the prayers would work, and other times, a death would rend all continuity for a while.

Time went on and the ravenous people who had spread throughout the lakes and plains below grew hungry again. They travelled up to the mountains seeking coal, and, finding it, promised they would not bother the mountain people as they satisfied their terrible appetites. The mountain people agreed to let the ravenous ones live among them, but quickly, as they had been warned by relatives and friends from farther away, the ravenous people multiplied and settled there. Promises

---

1 Isak Dinesen, as cited in Hannah Arendt, *The Human Condition* (Chicago: University of Chicago Press, 1958), 175.

were made and settlements built. In time, the mountain people came to learn that the ravenous people were both good and bad, both harsh and kind, just as among their own people. The only thing that distinguished them was their immobility and their unending appetite for accumulation.

Soon, a curious thing began to occur. While some mountain people flowed in and out from the bush, others settled into the routines of the ravenous ones, worked at their endeavours for money, even tried out and borrowed their habits and vices. Still others fluctuated back and forth, depending on the ease of the wage work, or the scarcity of game. A darkness settled upon the mountain people. A heaviness they could not explain soaked into their lives. Some began to try alcohol; some began to rely on it. The ravenous people built their ravenous schools and first invited the mountain people's children to spend their days learning their ravenous ways, then insisted that they come. Some of the ways were amazing: the ravenous peoples, being ravenous for everything, had much knowledge, from all parts of the world. Because the ravenous people accumulated, rather than shared, all their knowledge was jealously guarded by their language, in their particular works and structures. Slowly, the mountain people's children learned the language, the works, and structures. Slowly, the vast accumulated knowledge of the ravenous made the mountain people's children hesitate when they listened to the knowledge shared by their parents, their relatives. Some refused to speak the language of their parents, some took on the uncomfortable role of translator, endlessly explaining things to their parents as the ravenous ways endlessly encroached into their lives. Still others despaired. It was the long dark time.

Strange things happened in the long dark time. This is a story of Claire, a girl, when the dark time descended. Medicines did not always work in the dark time. Things that had always been true turned on their head. Claire grew up in the dark time, learning the ravenous people's accumulated knowledge, hesitating when she heard the language of her parents, which was comforting, but could not encompass all the knowledge she learned to gather, and spoke of knowledge that did not match the ravenous ways of knowing. Meanwhile, a strange dark shadow swept across the community. People would drink alcohol and shape shift into monsters, who did unspeakable things to those they loved. Children and adults learned to run and hide, learned to lock their doors when the transformations took place. But there was not always time, and it was so hard to see when someone you loved had turned;

the physical change was so subtle. Not surprisingly, children and adults would still get hurt, no matter how careful they were.

One day, when Claire was in that awkward in-between stage, not still a child but not yet a woman, she thought she saw her uncle coming to say hi, and didn't notice the tell-tale signs of the *wetiko* sickness, a subtle shift in his walking, messy hair, and the buttons on his shirt done up wrong – and maybe what looked like a bite mark on his lower lip. Before she could get away, he grabbed her and tore a chunk off her right arm. Claire would have screamed in pain, but she was in shock. This was her beloved uncle, and she had heard stories about him as a child, as a boy who made her mom laugh with his escapades, a boy who could mimic the sound of any animal alive. So instead she watched him chewing on her flesh, and felt the blood dripping from her arm, and wept. Finally, when he reached for her again, she came to her senses and ran from there. When she got home, she saw her mom's eye flicker to the gaping wound in her arm, saw the knowing there. She wished her mom would run to her and bandage the arm, but instead her mom turned her face away from the sight. Her mom could not bear to see the shape of her brother's teeth in her child's arm, the brother who made her laugh with his escapades and could mimic the sound of any animal alive. Next, Claire crept into her sister's room to ask her for help, but when her sister saw her wound she began to cry and simply pulled up her pant leg to reveal a similar wound, weeks old but still festering from lack of care, in the shape of their father's mouth. Claire reeled back in horror and ran from the house. She ran for a very, very long time, past the houses of everyone she knew and loved, past the ravenous people's homes, past the black smoking plant where they sucked up and devoured the very insides of the mountains.

At a last she came to a bank of a river, and exhausted, fell asleep. When she slept she dreamt. A very old woman sat beside her by the river, holding a crying baby. She seemed to be digging in the riverbank for something. Claire crept forward to watch. The old woman looked strangely familiar, like she had known her all her life. The old woman noticed her and smiled. "Ah," she said, "you've come to watch me now, after all these times I've been watching you." Claire didn't understand, but felt warm and safe, so smiled blearily. The old woman handed her the baby and finished what she was doing in the dirt. The baby screamed and struggled in Claire's arms, and she felt the ripping pain of the bite out of her right arm when she moved. She winced, and the old woman looked up at her in alarm. "Ah," she said sadly, "you are hurting then. What a horrible thing to have happen to you." She took the white dirt she had gathered in her hand and applied it to the baby's gums, who immediately stopped his wailing and slept. "Sweet dirt," she told Claire. "I wonder. Would it help you too with the pain from teeth?" She laid the baby down gently beside her. Carefully she poured water from the river over Claire's wound, and then packed it with the white dirt. "I don't know," she said, "maybe, maybe not. But that's all we can do for now. It is the time of darkness. It is the time of darkness," she said again, "but the darkness will not last forever. It is not all there is. We must remember that too."

Claire woke up alone by the river. There was no white dirt in the wound and there was no old woman. Her arm ached. She walked down to where she had seen the old woman digging in the bank, and sure enough, she saw the soft white dirt she had brought to her. Claire walked down to the river and washed her arm, just as the old woman had in her dream. Then she walked back up to the sweet dirt and packed it in the bite mark, just as the old woman had. It looked a bit funny, but it did seem to make the ache a bit less. She picked up another handful and put it in her pocket for later. She was all alone, but for some reason she didn't feel all alone anymore. She wondered if the old woman was watching her.

Claire walked back into her life, and her dad immediately smacked her on the face. "Your mom says you were playing around where you shouldn't," he said angrily. "What do you expect if you do things like that? From now on, just stay home." Claire thought about the bite wound on her sister's leg and ducked past him into the kitchen. Her mom was making supper and wouldn't look at her when she came in. Her sister was sitting at the table playing solitaire. Claire wanted to tell her sister about the sweet dirt, but her sister looked like she had been crying and wouldn't look up at her either. She slipped out the back door but she didn't feel like running anymore. She pulled her sleeve down to make sure the bite wound packed with sweet dirt didn't show, and she walked to go visit her cousin, Sky. Sky was always laughing, and right then she was laughing over a comic she was reading. Claire settled in beside her and was amazed to find herself laughing too. Here she had thought she might never laugh again, only earlier that day. A little later that day she rolled over on the grass and caught sight of a bite mark on Sky's skinny ankle. She felt sad, but the memory of the old woman and the laughter from the comic book was still with her. She told Sky the whole story, of her bite, her dream, the old woman, and the sweet dirt. Sky looked like she didn't know quite what to think, but when Claire pulled the leftover white dirt from her pocket, soft as silk, she wept, and they covered her wound with it too. That was a good day for Claire and Sky.

Five years later, Claire's scar from that bite mark had healed so that it barely showed, but it hardly mattered anymore. Since that summer day with her cousin, Sky, she had been bitten at least five more times. The first time she limped down to the river, washed the bite mark, and dug some more of the sweet dirt up for it, but the second time she couldn't bring herself to go that far. By the third time, she cried for the old woman, but when she appeared in her dream, Claire screamed at her, angry she was there, watching, but not stopping the monstrous happenings. The fourth time she hardly felt the teeth anymore, even though there was a pack. The fifth time, she was offered a half bottle of cheap booze and she chugged it back. The sweet dirt had dulled the ache, but alcohol numbed it completely, at least for a time. One day she cried in the ravenous school and was sent to a nurse, who looked over all her terrible bites and red eyes and pronounced her a crying shame, but sadly typical for the mountain people's children. She got in a fight soon after that and was mercifully expelled.

There was always someone with alcohol, and with enough alcohol, she could laugh again, like that summer day with her cousin, Sky. She could stave off the searing pain from the bites that never seemed to heal over, and she could sometimes vent the terrible rage that seemed to have its own life inside of her. One day, she woke up from a three-day binge and saw her own teeth marks on a child's arm. She couldn't think of anything. By that point she barely remembered that day by the river. She wanted to say sorry to the little one, but she remembered enough to know that she herself would not have wanted such an encounter, so instead she went looking for a drink. Claire's life went on after that, but it stopped being much of a story. Sometimes, the best you can say is that things continue on – over and over again, like an old record with a deep scratch in it. Once in a while, Claire would wake up and think she saw an old woman weeping over her, or watching her from a distance, and once in a while, something so horrific would happen to Claire, or be done by her, that the world would seem to stop, prepared to change the direction of the story, but then the pain would well up, and her old familiar habits would bear down.

Sky remembered that day in the summer, when she was eleven years old, reading a comic. She would think about the story of the old woman and the sweet dirt. Sometimes she would look at the spot on her leg where they had put the sweet dirt, and marvel at how smooth the skin was – almost as if the bite left no mark at all. Other times she would get annoyed at her cousin when she would come over, always trying to borrow money from her, asking her to help her out of this or that situation, asking so much she felt surely she had paid back all the benefits from the sweet dirt years ago. But still, she would feel the skin over the scar and help her out. One time, she tried to ask her about the old woman, but Claire was snarly from needing a drink and sneered at her. "If you want her you can have her, watching over us, doing nothing."

Sky felt bad, and a little embarrassed, but that night she dreamed of the old woman for the first time. She was exactly as Claire had described her, all those years ago, but maybe a little older than she had imagined. The old woman looked happy to see her. With a twinkle in her eye, she told Sky, "Now don't go thinking you can just foist me off on each other. I'm grandmother to both of you. But maybe Claire's right, I should start doing a little more for you girls, but she's in no shape to hear anymore." A tear trickled down her face. "In no shape to help anyone anymore. But she helped you, didn't she? That was good, that's what we're supposed to do. Your niece Anna," the old woman went on, "she got bitten by Claire, when Claire got taken over by the *wetiko* sickness last year. Maybe you can go bring her some of the sweet dirt – it's still where it's always been." And in the dream, the old woman took Sky's hand and took her to the river, showed her the spot where Claire had dug in the bank so many years ago, showed her the soft white dirt inside the brown bank.

The next day, Sky called in sick to work and walked all the way to the river. She recognized the spot from her dream and began to dig. Soon she had filled a jar with the soft white dirt, and once it was full, she walked home with it. There was a lot of sweet dirt in the jar, and she remembered it took so little of it to soothe her own damaged skin so long ago. There was a lot she could do with a jar full of sweet dirt, she reflected. Then again, there were a lot of people in the community who were hurting. She wasn't sure, once she thought of them all, if even the whole jar would be enough. The other thing was that Claire had the dream, used the sweet dirt, but kept getting bitten, so it alone couldn't be enough. They would have to be like the ravenous people and mine the whole riverbank, and once it was all gone, it would be all gone.

She decided she would share the story and some of the sweet dirt with her young niece Anna, like the old woman suggested, but other than that, she would put it away and think about what to do with it.

That's what she did. That very night Anna came visiting and Sky could see the old woman was right. Her eyes had that frightened, ashamed look, somewhere between the look of a prisoner and a scared rabbit, and she was holding her left arm in a funny way, wearing three shirts instead of one, trying to hide what had happened, trying to protect herself from it happening again. Sky was going to tell her the story, but one look at her face and she knew she had to get the girl laughing a bit first, feed her some supper, remind her about all the good and warm things in life. That's what she did, and after their bellies were full and Anna was giggling from all the funniest stories Sky could remember, Sky told her about the old woman, Claire, and the sweet dirt. Anna was really quiet. "Claire gave it to you," she said softly. "I don't know if it would work on me, I don't know if I want something from her." And that scared rabbit/prisoner look came back in her eyes all of sudden. Sky could have kicked herself for mentioning Claire, but then, she thought carefully, she was telling Anna the truth. That's where they were now, all together, where someone could bring such healing and such pain in the same lifetime.

Finally she spoke: "I know what Claire did to you, and it wasn't right. She's my cousin, and she gave me quite the gift when I was about your age. Plus, we used to laugh our heads off together. And the stuff she's been through, I wouldn't wish on my worst enemy. I guess the thing with pain is, when we pass it on, it multiplies itself. That's what she's done, letting herself be taken over by the *wetiko* spirit, doing to you what was done to her. It wasn't your fault. It was hers. And," Sky added, "I guess I see why it doesn't make sense that something that harmful and something healing could ever come to you through the same source." Anna didn't say anything, just looked at Sky. "If you ever want some," Sky said, "it's right here on my shelf. It's not from Claire, you know, she was just the one who got told about it. If it's from anyone, it's from the river; it's from our grandmother." Anna didn't say anything, just looked at Sky.

Sky couldn't tell you if Anna ever took some of the sweet dirt or not. She came and visited Sky a lot, all through her teenage years, even when most of her friends were too busy experimenting with oblivion and other arts. Sometimes she would bring a friend with her and sometimes she came alone. She even babysat for Sky once in a while. Sky fed her and made her laugh and told her stories about people and places they both knew. Sky's own children grew bright and strong, and Anna seemed to be growing stronger and brighter every year too. A strength seemed to grow in Sky as they grew, to stand up for them when she had to. She did so many times. Through the years there were days when Sky was so tired she would cry, and days she was so sad she just wanted to sleep forever. But she kept doing what she did every day for her kids, for Anna, for the generations ahead of them all. Sometimes Sky would dream of their grandmother, smiling, walking beside her by the river, saying, "I feel the brightness coming back to us now." Sometimes, between monsters walking and the ravenous people's persistent battering, Sky couldn't see past the darkness in the daytime, but in those dreams, she could feel the brightness too.

Chapter 1

Introduction and Methodology

Speaking the Unspeakable

A long, long time ago, in a time of starvation, a man tried to go hunting. First he saw a wolverine, but when he was going to kill it, he couldn't, because he saw the frozen face of a child who had died in the last year between its toes. Then he saw a lynx, and there again he saw the frozen face of another child between its toes. He was full of grief for the children and could not kill the lynx either, even though everyone was starving. When he got home, he told the elders about what he saw. The elders listened and guessed a *wetiko* was after him. One told him, "He's trying to cause those deaths over again, with you!" The man realized they were right, and set out again with other hunters to kill the *wetiko*. As they walked by the wolverine and the lynx, they all "grieved again to themselves, both times." Despite this, they kept going as a group. In the end, they finally caught the *wetiko* and melted his heart.[1]

When I first went to law school, sometimes I too felt as if I could not take what I was supposed to because of the frozen faces of children that I kept seeing. Like the hunters, I grieved again and again to myself as I passed them. It is these faces and this grieving that led me to the *wetiko* stories. Nowadays, many Indigenous people are grieving. They are grieving the memories of children and adults lost to violence and victimization, both from the residential schools and within

---

1 Howard Norman, *Where the Chill Came From: Cree Windigo Tales and Journeys* (San Francisco: North Point, 1982), 42.

communities.[2] It's hard to think about what has happened to so many of our children. It's hard to look at what is happening to our children today. The level of violence within some Indigenous communities is overwhelming.[3] It is a constant struggle to cope with the resulting horror, loss, and grief.

The violence is bad enough. But today, the violence is often both caused by and felt by those close to us. How do we speak about the unspeakable?[4] How do we protect those we love, *from* those we love? How do we respond as a community to such harm and horror? Communities face hopelessness and despair, as if there is no way out of a dark time; as if all our efforts are pointless; as if, as parents, grandparents, aunties, and uncles, we are powerless to stop the pain from

---

2 This violence and victimization has been referred to as the "legacy" of the residential schools. The Aboriginal Healing Foundation (http://www.ahf.ca/about-us/mission) describes its mission as supporting the healing needs from the "legacy of abuse" from the residential schools. "The legacy" is used extensively throughout Schedule N of the Indian Residential Schools Settlement Agreement, http://www.residentialschoolsettlement.ca/SCHEDULE_N.pdf. Some theorists argue massive, intergenerational trauma goes beyond the residential schools themselves, and is part of the social upheaval caused deliberately or blindly by colonial mechanisms. For example, see John Borrows, "Crown and Aboriginal Occupations of Land: A History & Comparison," research paper prepared for the Ipperwash Inquiry (2005), section 2 (57–76), https://www.attorneygeneral.jus.gov.on.ca/inquiries/ipperwash/policy_part/research/pdf/History_of_Occupations_Borrows.pdf; and James B. Waldram, Revenge of the Windigo: The Construction of the Mind and Mental Health of North American Aboriginal Peoples (Toronto: University of Toronto Press, 2004), 225.

3 A report commissioned by the Aboriginal Healing Foundation concludes, "All available evidence suggests the rates of violence and sexual offending in many Aboriginal communities are … as much as five times higher than Canadian rates, perhaps higher." See John H. Hylton, *Aboriginal Sexual Offending in Canada*, 2nd ed. (Ottawa: Aboriginal Healing Foundation, 2006), 69, http://www.ahf.ca/publications/research-series. Mary Ellen Turpel-Lafond states, "The pressing reality is that we have unprecedented levels of violence experienced in Aboriginal families and communities in the current generation, likely connected to the intergenerational trauma from the residential school experience." See Mary Ellen Turpel-Lafond, "Some Thoughts on Inclusion and Innovation in the Saskatchewan Justice System," *Saskatchewan Law Review* 68 (2005): 295. See also Rupert Ross, "Traumatization in Remote First Nations: An Expression of Concern" (2006), author's collection.

4 In her seminal work on trauma and recovery, Judith Herman begins by explaining, "The ordinary response to atrocities is to banish them from consciousness. Certain violations of the social compact are too terrible to utter aloud: this is the very meaning of the word *unspeakable*. Atrocities however, refuse to be buried." Judith Herman, *Trauma and Recovery: The Aftermath of Violence; From Domestic Violence to Political Terror* (New York: Basic Books, 1997), 1.

spreading to the next generation; as if there is no hope. We seem frozen in our sadness. It is this situation that led me to the *wetiko* stories.

There are many *wetiko* stories, spanning hundreds of years, in Cree and Anishinabek societies. The earliest stories are about cannibal giants or spirits, like the one above, and how the people faced this horror and danger. There are also stories about strangers who are suspected of cannibalism. Many stories involve people who are known and loved who cause terrible harm to themselves or others. This can include stealing, hoarding, murder, and cannibalism. This may seem horrific, but some of the violence occurring today is even more horrific.[5] Some stories are about a person in the process of becoming a *wetiko*. These people might act "strange," make threats, appear depressed, withdraw, isolate themselves, hurt themselves, stop taking care of themselves, try to hurt or bite others, look for weapons, or do things they can't remember later. Most people becoming a *wetiko* were cured, but when healing didn't work, and they became more dangerous, groups and medicine people worked together to keep others safe, even if the only option left was death.

Sadly, in the past, Canadian government and courts, as well as academics and newspapers, have used the *wetiko* stories to say Indigenous people were superstitious, brutal, or uncivilized. In extreme cases, Indigenous people who had to kill a *wetiko* to protect others were tried for murder and jailed or hanged. This happened even though everyone in their community said they acted according to their law. Some people may believe that if we talk about the *wetiko*, one will come. The past has taught people that talking about the *wetiko* can be dangerous. Other people just don't see any use for these stories today. For all these reasons, many people may feel cautious, ashamed, or doubtful about using the *wetiko* stories today. I agree we should be careful, but I do not think anyone should feel ashamed. The *wetiko* stories are powerful examples of Cree and Anishinabek peoples' profound strength, resourcefulness, and teamwork in protecting themselves and those they love. Some medicine people still heal people turning into a *wetiko* today. This strength is still with us.

We need these stories. We need them for thinking through what we face today. This includes facing the violence and victimization within communities – intimate violence, child sexual victimization, all kinds of violence fed by drugs, alcohol, and gangs, and the senseless violence increasingly committed by youth themselves, children no longer

---

5 See, e.g., Ross, "Traumatization in Remote First Nations," 1–4.

capable of feeling anything at all.[6] This violence erases lives and eats up our strength. Too often it leaves us numb or divided in our grief. In addition, when people reach out for help or a tragedy ends up in the news, the worst kinds of personal trauma are often reduced to the belittling stereotypes of the "sick" or the "savage."[7] This insult heaped on injury – humiliation added to already deep wounds – can feed back into anger, isolation, and paralysis. Where to turn? One place is the strengths and resources within communities themselves.

This book focuses on one part of building towards a healthier future: identifying and building on internal strengths and resources.[8] This is not about self-blame, false hope, or easy answers. Certainly, there are no quick fixes to the current situation. Any long-term fix requires attention

---

6 Ross reports seeing "an escalating number of young people whose exposure to violence at home and in the community has rendered them incapable of feeling either empathy for others or remorse for their own actions." Ibid., 4.

7 See especially the treatment of child welfare and justice issues in Frances Widdowson and Albert Howard, *Disrobing the Aboriginal Industry: The Deception behind Indigenous Cultural Preservation* (Montreal and Kingston: McGill-Queen's University Press, 2008), 158–72. For examples of news articles discussing individual tragedies as examples of a much larger dysfunction in Indigenous communities, see Paula Simon, "Relatives Not Automatically Best Caregivers for Child in Need," *Edmonton Journal*, 31 January 2009; and *National Post*, "The Verdict on Sentencing Circles," 18 February 2009, http://www.pressreader.com/canada/national-post-latest-edition/20090218/281822869698430.

8 The choice for this focus comes from two directions. One is political. See the argument that Indigenous peoples should "turn away" from the dominant society to focus on a critical individual and collective "self-recognition," in Glen S. Coulthard, "Subjects of the Empire: Indigenous Peoples and the 'Politics of Recognition' in Canada," *Contemporary Political Theory* 6 (2007): 456; and the critical questions asked in Val Napoleon, Angela Cameron, Colette Arcand, and Dahti Scott, "Where's the Law in Restorative Justice?" in *Aboriginal Self-Government in Canada: Current Trends and Issues*, ed. Yale Belanger, 3rd ed. (Saskatoon: Purich Publishing, 2008), 3: "What are we beyond our resistance to colonialism? What do we want our contemporary legal institutions and laws to look like?" The other direction is pragmatic. Two key trends in *prevention* of child victimization are (1) promoting resiliency by enhancing "protective factors or strengths" and (2) competency based, solution-focused practice, where practitioners identify and build on strengths and capabilities, rather than focusing on skill deficits and weaknesses. See Rex Wild and Patricia Anderson, "Part II: Supporting Research," in *Ampe Akelyernemane Meke Mekarle, "Little Children Are Sacred": Report of the Northern Territory Board of Inquiry into the Protection of Aboriginal Children from Sexual Abuse* (Darwin, AU: Northern Territory Government, 2007), s. 9.3.

to the larger political issues of lost land, entrenched generational poverty, systemic racism, and racist violence within the dominant society.[9] However, there is also power within communities to think and act in the meantime. The actions of people in the *wetiko* stories show how people work together in a principled, effective way to face violence and danger created by community members. I believe these principled ways of responding to terrible harm can be seen as part of Cree and Anishinabek *law*. Some people still practise this law. We can draw on these people's knowledge and experience, as well as the experiences from the past, to see how they might apply today in broader circumstances.

Indigenous law can be hard to see when we are used to seeing law as something the Canadian government or police make or do. Some people may have even been taught that Indigenous people did not have law before white people came here. This is a lie. Law can be found in how groups deal with safety, how they make decisions and solve problems together, and what we expect people "should" do in certain situations (their *obligations*).[10] Some people say Indigenous laws can be found in stories, dreams, dances, art, in the world around us and in how we live our lives. Some people say they are "written on our hearts."[11] They

---

9 The need to address these broader issues should not be underestimated. Many writers and reports stress this. See Marlee Kline, "Child Welfare Law, 'Best Interests of the Child' Ideology, and First Nations," *Osgoode Hall Law Journal* 30 (1992): 425; Amnesty International, *Stolen Sisters: A Human Rights Approach to Discrimination and Violence against Indigenous Women in Canada* (2004), 2, 11, 19, and 29, https://www.amnesty.ca/sites/amnesty/files/amr200032004enstolensisters.pdf; Elizabeth Adjin-Tettey, "Sentencing Aboriginal Offenders: Balancing Offenders' Needs, the Interests of Victims and Society, and the Process of Decolonization of Aboriginal Peoples," *Canadian Journal of Women and the Law* 19 (2007): 199; Wendy Stewart, Audrey Huntley, and Fay Blaney, *The Implications of Restorative Justice for Aboriginal Women and Children Survivors of Violence: A Comparative Overview of Five Communities in British Columbia* (Ottawa: Law Commission of Canada, 2001), chap. 4, 4; Emma LaRocque, "Re-examining Culturally Appropriate Models of Criminal Justice," in *Aboriginal and Treaty Rights in Canada*, ed. Michael Asch (Vancouver: UBC Press, 1997), 86; and John Borrows, Maureen Maloney, and Dawnis Kennedy, *An Assessment of the Interrelationship between Economic and Justice Strategies in Urban Aboriginal Communities* (Victoria, BC: University of Victoria, Institute for Dispute Resolution and Faculty of Law, 2005) [Urban Aboriginal Report], 1:19–22.
10 The legal theory behind these three characteristics will be discussed further in chapter 2.
11 Law Commission of Canada, *Justice Within, Indigenous Legal Traditions*, DVD (Ottawa: Minister of Supply and Services Canada, 2006).

are often practised and passed down through individuals, families, and ceremonies.[12] This is why many still survive, after all the government efforts to stop them and sneer at them.[13] Because of the presence of Canadian law, and the lies and efforts to stop Indigenous law, some Indigenous laws are sleeping. It is time to awaken them.

Some people talk about the *wetiko* as strictly a psychological concept, or as a spiritual concept. I am going to talk about the *wetiko* as a legal concept or category. I will talk about an "ideal type" (a pure or simple form of) *wetiko* as a cannibal, and I will talk about the *wetiko* as a broad legal concept – a category that covers more behaviours than actually killing and eating other people. This includes many terrible ways people are dangerous and harmful to themselves and others. We can use the "ideal type" *wetiko* – the cannibal, as an analogy (something that is the same as, or similar to something else) for people who use, harm, or destroy others to satisfy their own appetites or wants. Or we can think about the destructive and often horrific violence and victimization described above as a behaviour that fits within a broad *wetiko* legal category.

I am going to talk about *legal principles* in the *wetiko* stories. Legal principles are rules, but they are not necessarily strict and unbending. Instead, they are like signposts that guide our thinking and actions. Legal principles can be about legal obligations – responsibilities, or what people "should" do – or about rights – what people should be able to expect from others. For example, a legal obligation in the *wetiko* stories might be that people should protect others from a *wetiko* if they can. A legal right might be that a person who asks for help for or with a *wetiko* should be able to expect someone to provide that help. Legal principles can also be about *legal processes*, like how a group solves problems together, who figures out what the rules mean and how they should be applied or adapted in the present situation. For example, a legal process connected to the above *legal obligation* could be about how the group decides on the best way to protect others from a *wetiko*, or who decides, by what standards, whether people did the best they could to protect others. A legal process connected to the above *legal right* could be figuring out who could best help and how this can happen safely and fairly.

---

12 John Borrows, *Canada's Indigenous Constitution* (Toronto: University of Toronto Press, 2010), 248.
13 Ibid.

In summary, I think the *wetiko* legal principles about legal obligations and processes may be useful tools for

1 thinking about how to protect our children from terrible harms caused by people close to us, and
2 thinking about how to recognize and respond to people close to us who may cause terrible harm to others.

I am interested in what we can learn about these subjects in the *wetiko* stories.

A Note on Methodology

As part of the research for this book, I interviewed Cree elders and community members in northern Alberta. There were two main purposes for the interviews. The first was to fill in the glaring gaps in non-Indigenous *wetiko* accounts. Most written accounts fail to discuss the reasoning by the Indigenous people responding to someone becoming or almost becoming a *wetiko* or any long-term implications of this situation, although it seems obvious there must be both.[14] The second purpose of the interviews was to have conversations about how I am interpreting and applying the *wetiko* stories as legal resources with people familiar with the stories themselves, who live and think within the larger normative frameworks (guiding standards for conduct) of which these stories are just one part. Put simply, I needed to know if my interpretations made sense in a contemporary northern Cree context,[15] because if they don't, the whole project is essentially pointless. For this reason, I was primarily seeking normative conversations, rather than empirical information from interviewees. It was about the discussion itself, as much as the data.

I conducted the interviews in a northern Alberta community I have been connected to for twenty-five years, as a friend, a mother, and an auntie, and in which I originally heard stories about *wetiko*s. Everyone I interviewed knows me. I prepared the interview packages, and the

---

14 This was obviously a qualitative, rather than a quantitative approach to these research questions.
15 This does not mean I sought complete agreement with my book, because part of all law is reasoned disagreement and varying interpretations. However, differing viewpoints must still make sense within a given context.

person who agreed to translate discussed them with the elders and asked whether they wanted to participate well in advance of the official consent and interview process. This indirect method was to give the elders time to think and to avoid putting them in a situation where they might feel pressured. I approached the interviews relationally, beginning with elders who are my in-laws and close family friends, and relying on their referrals for further interviews. In this way, I remained accountable to them, as well as to the university's ethical standards for research.

Interviews took place in people's homes, generally over several hours, with at least one or two other family members present, all of whom also asked questions and discussed the stories whenever they wanted to. This open, conversational setting was very similar to the original settings in which I heard these stories. My translator, Carol Wanyandie, an extremely intelligent and intuitive person, asked her own questions as they arose, which led to several insightful and interesting connections I hadn't thought of asking about. I interviewed three elders, three adult and two young adult community members. While people spoke openly within the community, everyone I interviewed asked to remain anonymous for the written version. This wish has been respected by referring to interviewees as elders or community members.[16]

In addition to the oral descriptions and discussions of people's recent actions and reasoning from these interviews, I will draw on ancient stories and written descriptive accounts of people's past actions. In the ancient stories, *wetiko*s are usually giants. In these stories, the tricksters, Wesakaychak (Cree) and Nanabush (Anishinabek), encounter *wetiko*s; animals and people talk to each other; and one way people find or fight the *wetiko* is by "conjuring." The written and oral descriptive accounts of people's past and recent actions describe people who have become, or are in the process of becoming, a *wetiko*. Some people still use medicine or spiritual means, or are helped by non-human life forms. Some stories may be difficult to believe or understand for some readers. For example, written descriptions by white observers are incomplete and often reflect the writer's beliefs that Indigenous people are ignorant or incapable. These descriptions do not match

---

16 This relatively small number was due to my own time constraints. Everyone I asked did agree to be interviewed, and I simply did not have the time to follow up on the rest of the suggested interviewees. This may be an area for further or follow-up research. At the time of publication, elders Adelaide McDonald and Norman McDonald chose to be named rather than remain anonymous.

what Indigenous people know about themselves and from their own experiences. It is good to be cautious, and readers should not need to accept the truth of something they do not believe to draw on the *wetiko* legal principles. This is one reason I have triangulated sources – in other words, looked at many stories, from all three sources, rather than relying on just one.

I have intentionally written this book to be valid and reliable enough for an academic audience but also be readable for a non-academic audience. I hope people in the community who may be interested in the *wetiko* legal principles can also read it. For that reason, I have made my best attempt to use plain language, and use footnotes for theoretical discussions.[17] This book begins and ends with a story. What is between the stories? The second chapter will explain why I think the *wetiko* can be seen as a legal concept. It is geared towards an academic audience, and focuses on legal theory and methodology. If you are not interested in legal theory, it can be skipped. The third chapter will build on the idea that the *wetiko* is a legal concept. It will talk about how the ways that people think or theorize about *wetiko* dynamics are *analogous* (similar) to how we now think or theorize about the dynamics of offenders and child victimization. The fourth chapter will explain the *wetiko* legal principles about people's legal obligations, rights, and processes in relation to a *wetiko*. The fifth and final chapter will suggest possible next steps for researching the future challenges and uses for these legal principles.

Although I do not know very much at all,[18] what follows is my best understanding of what the *wetiko* legal principles may teach us about thinking through some of the painful things Indigenous communities face today.

---

17 While this is an academic book, I want these words to be accessible to those I wrote them for, and who took such care to make these principles accessible to me in the first place.

18 Introducing the rest of the project this way is in keeping with the way many elders begin to speak about what they know, and open-endedness of narratives within Cree society. See Neal McLeod, *Cree Narrative Memory: From Treaties to Contemporary Times* (Saskatoon: Purich Publishing, 2007), 12–13. This traditional opening resonates with me, because I continue to learn how little I actually know, and because it reinforces the importance of individual interpretation and internalization of all narratives (13).

Chapter 2

The *Wetiko* as a Legal Concept or Category

Framing the Inquiry: The Where and the What of the *Wetiko*

I have known a windigo; he was my cook in the tundra. He made excellent bread, but I cared less for his meat sauces.[1]

The epigraph, written, one presumes, tongue-in-cheek, captures the fact that accounts of the *wetiko*[2] stories are always listened to and retold for specific purposes, and interpreted within specific frames of reference.[3] It also slyly alludes to the aspect of the *wetiko* stories that have primarily garnered the attentions of non-Indigenous scholars and legal

---

1 Jean-Jacques Rousseau, quoted in Morton Teicher, "Windigo Psychosis: A Study of a Relationship between Belief and Behavior among the Indians of Northeastern Canada," in *Proceedings of the 1960 Annual Spring Meeting of the American Ethnological Society*, ed. Verne F. Ray (Seattle: University of Washington Press, 1960), 80.

2 I use the spelling *Wetiko* throughout this book for consistency, and because it is the simplest phonetic spelling of the Cree pronunciation I am most familiar with. Where I quote other writers I use their spelling. However, there are also diverse spellings of this term, including *windigo, wendigo, wintego, wihtego, windego, wendago, wintigo, wintsigo, wehtigoo, windagoo, windikouk, weendigo, wentiko, wiitiko, whittico, weendegoag, weendago*, and *weetigo*. Morton Teicher, "Windigo Psychosis: A Study of a Relationship between Belief and Behavior among the Indians of Northeastern Canada," in *Proceedings of the 1960 Annual Spring Meeting of the American Ethnological Society*, ed. Verne F. Ray (Seattle: University of Washington Press, 1960), 2.

3 All narratives are "constantly being reinterpreted and recreated in light of shifting experience and context." Neal McLeod, *Cree Narrative Memory: From Treaties to Contemporary Times* (Saskatoon: Purich Publishing, 2007), ii.

actors: in many accounts, *wetiko* is a synonym for cannibal. Of course, this is also the case in many of the more dramatic and entertaining stories on this subject told by Indigenous people.[4] However, it is clear, from both the academic literature and the interviews conducted for this project, that the term *wetiko* is used for a broader range of behaviours than just actual cannibalism. As we shall see in this section, various academics postulate different theories for this breadth of use. After a review of the work of the key theorists in this area, as well as the oral information shared in interviews for this project, I have concluded that the *wetiko* concept is multifaceted, and that the simplest explanation for this complexity is to understand the term *wetiko* as a complex intellectual concept within certain Indigenous societies. The subject matter, the collective reasoning processes, and the obligations that are triggered by its use all suggest it is best understood as a *legal* concept. Reconceptualized in this way, the *wetiko* accounts can be re-analysed and applied as part of certain northern Indigenous legal traditions.

Stories about the *wetiko* are part of oral traditions in at least northern Cree and Anishinabek societies. Some writers have pointed out that there are very similar concepts in other Indigenous societies[5] and among non-Indigenous populations as well.[6] Stories about the *wetiko* were sometimes recorded as collections of folklore or mythology.[7] There are also a number of Euro-Canadian historical accounts of events that involve Indigenous and non-Indigenous responses to *wetiko*-related

---

4 My particular favourite is the *wetiko* who killed 500 people, who freeze at the sound of his cry. When they are frozen, he goes around chopping off heads, then their buttocks! He roasts the people, but hangs their butts up to dry around their camp before moving on, as trophies. That's how people know he killed that many people. This story was told to me with much laughter. Interview 1: Interview of Adelaide McDonald and Norman McDonald, 11 April 2009, Alberta.

5 See Robin Ridington, "Wechuge and Windigo: A Comparison of Cannibal Belief among Boreal Forest Athapaskans and Algonquians," in *Little Bit Know Something: Stories in the Language of Anthropology* (Vancouver: Douglas and McIntyre, 1990), 160; and Raymond D. Fogelson, "Windigo Goes South: Stoneclad among the Cherokees," in *Manlike Monsters on Trial: Early Records and Modern Evidence*, ed. Marjorie Halpin and Michael M. Ames (Vancouver: UBC Press, 1980), 132.

6 Carolyn Podruchny, "Werewolves and Windigos: Narratives of Cannibal Monsters in French-Canadian Voyageur Tradition," *Ethnohistory* 5, no. 4 (2004): 677.

7 See Candice Savage, ed., *The World of Wetiko: Tales from the Woodland Cree, as Told by Marie Merasty* (Saskatoon, SK: Saskatchewan Indian Cultural College, 1974); Howard Norman, *Where the Chill Came From: Cree Windigo Tales and Journeys* (San Francisco: North Point, 1982); and first part of Teicher, "Windigo Psychosis," 17–43.

anxieties and behaviours. These include journals and other writing by missionaries, explorers, and employees of the Hudson Bay Company,[8] as well as government documents and court records about the arrests, trials, or treatment of people accused of murder in relation to *wetiko* executions.[9] In addition to these sources, there is also a body of anthropological and psychological academic literature.

Typical characteristics of a person who had become a *wetiko* in older oral stories and recorded accounts are striking and often grotesque. A *wetiko* "literally ate its own lips."[10] It also "lost the instinct to keep clean: its hair was long, shaggy, matted and full of dirt …; its body went unwashed; its teeth discolored; its finger- and toe-nails grew long and broke off. Its clothes were dirty, smelly and sometimes so tattered the *Wetiko* roamed almost naked."[11]

Many stories and recorded accounts include swelling, incoherency, and threats, as well as enormous strength[12] and supernatural powers, including floating above the ground[13] and a paralysing yell.[14] Often people described a patch of ice[15] or "chunk of green stuff" on the *wetiko*'s

---

8 See Jennifer S.H. Brown and Robert Brightman, *The Orders of the Dreamed: George Nelson on Cree and Northern Ojibwa Religion and Myth, 1923* (Winnipeg: University of Manitoba Press, 1990).

9 See *R v Machekequonabe* [1897] OJ No 98, 2 CCC 138 (the only such reported case); the police and court materials regarding the case of Swift Runner, a Cree man charged and hanged for murder after evidence was found he killed and ate his children and wife, as replicated in Teicher, "Windigo Psychosis," 85–8; the arrest and trial of several Cree men charged with murder for executing a man named Moostoos, who appeared to have become a *wetiko*, as replicated in ibid., 93–103; the arrest and trial of Jack and Joseph Fiddler, shaman and chief of the Sucker Clan, accused and convicted of murder for executing a woman who appeared to have become a *wetiko*, in Thomas Fiddler and James R. Stevens, *Killing the Shaman* (Newcastle, ON: Penumbra, 1991).

10 Savage, *World of Wetiko*, 3; and Interview #1. An elder's adult son told one story about a female *wetiko* who ate her breasts as well. It was explained that any part of their flesh they could reach, they would eat, including bites out of their arms and hands.

11 Savage, *World of Wetiko*, 3.

12 Teicher, "Windigo Psychosis," 93.

13 Ibid.; and Interview 4: Interview of anonymous community member, 13 April 2009, Alberta.

14 Interview 1; Interview 4. Once people were frozen by the yell, the *wetiko* would kill them as he liked. In one story, they were killed with a dull axe. Interview 1.

15 Savage, *World of Wetiko*, 3.

back[16] or in his or her stomach.[17] When people were "turning *wetiko*" they would stop eating and refuse any food offered to them.[18] They might isolate themselves[19] or become consumed with "sad thoughts" or "melancholia."[20]

Cannibalism was "often, but not always" one aspect of "going [*wetiko*]."[21] Importantly, *wetiko* was used to describe cannibalism, but also used to describe "only a murderer of his fellows, urged on by dreams, melancholy, and brooding,"[22] or an "evil person or spirit who terrorizes other creatures by means of terrible evil acts."[23] Cannibalistic ideation was often cited as both a precursor to someone becoming a *wetiko*,[24] and a continuing obsession that contributed to the repetition of the offence. Some people believed that "once a person had eaten human flesh, he found other foods distasteful."[25] Often, though, obsessions about eating other people,[26] including dreams[27] or hallucinations of other people as animals acceptable to eat, were seen as precursors or danger signals

---

16 Teicher, "Windigo Psychosis," 57.

17 Interview 2: Interview of anonymous elder, 13 April 2009, Alberta; and Brown and Brightman, "On Windigo Psychosis," 93.

18 Teicher, "Windigo Psychosis," 64.

19 Interview 4.

20 J.B. Tyrell, ed., *David Thompson's Narratives* (1916), 125–6, in Teicher, "Windigo Psychosis," 81.

21 Norman, *Where the Chill Came From*, 3.

22 Ibid.

23 Jack D. Forbes, *Columbus and Other Cannibals: The Wetiko Disease of Exploitation, Imperialism and Terrorism*, rev. ed. (Toronto: Seven Stories, 2008), 24. Forbes says the noun *wetikowatisewin* can refer to either "diabolical wickedness or cannibalism."

24 See Henry Y. Hind, *Explorations in the Interior of the Labrador Peninsula* (London: Longman, Green, Longman, Roberts and Green, 1863), in Teicher, "Windigo Psychosis," 103.

25 Savage, *World of Wetiko*, 3.

26 See Brown and Brightman, *Orders of the Dreamed*, 91–2, where a father says to his daughter, "Yes! I love thee – I think I could eat a piece of thee, I love thee so much," then "puts himself stark naked and uttering a strong tremulous noise" and slept outside, "curled as a dog in a heap." He would not eat, except a little raw flesh, and this continued for some time.

27 For example, M. Duncan Cameron, *The Nipigon Country* (1804), in *Les Bourgeois de la Campagne du Nord-Ouest*, ed. L.R. Masson (Quebec: A. Coté, 1890), 249–50, in Teicher, "Windigo Psychosis," 104; and Brown and Brightman, *Orders of the Dreamed*, 90. As will become clear later on, I disagree with the conclusion that it was believed dreams predestined someone to become a *wetiko*.

that someone was becoming a *wetiko*.[28] In one case dealt with under Canadian law, Swift Runner, a Cree man in Alberta, was executed upon the discovery of the boiled and burned bones of his entire family. Upon confrontation, he confessed to killing and eating them all and was hanged.[29] While cannibalism is perhaps the most salacious and dramatic aspect of many *wetiko* stories, a preponderance of evidence in the literature and oral recollections shows that cannibalism alone fails to capture the actual historical or contemporary complexity of the term.

Reconceptualizing the Literature: The *Wetiko* as an Intellectual Concept

Much of the academic debate over the *wetiko* has largely been about the existence or non-existence of a disorder called "windigo psychosis" that included cannibalistic ideation and behaviour, and corresponding explanations of this "culturally bound" phenomenon.[30] It is worthwhile reviewing three of the key anthropological contributors to this debate: Morton Teicher, Lou Marano, and Robert Brightman, as they have collected the most data and conducted the most thorough academic analyses of the *wetiko* concept. Although each of these scholars offers different theories, they all demonstrate, through their data, if not their final analysis, the historical complexity of the *wetiko* concept.

Morton Teicher is well known for his collection and analysis of several *wetiko* myths and seventy *wetiko* cases spanning 300 years involving

---

28 See Teicher, "Windigo Psychosis," 59, 76, and 89–90. See also Norman, *Where the Chill Came From*, 4, citing Isaac Grays, a Cree elder.

29 J.P. Turner, *The Northwest Mounted Police* (1950), 499–501, in Teicher, "Windigo Psychosis," 85.

30 See Teicher, "Windigo Psychosis"; the seminal article by Lou Marano et al., "Windigo Psychosis: The Anatomy of an Emic-Etic Confusion [and Comments and Reply]," *Current Anthropology* 23, no. 4 (1982): 385–412; Robert Brightman, "The Windigo in the Material World," *Ethnohistory* 35, no. 4 (1988): 337–79; Robert Brightman, David Meyer, and Lou Marano, "On Windigo Psychosis," *Current Anthropology* 21, no. 1 (1983): 120–5; Richard J. Preston, "The Wetiko: Algonquian Knowledge and Whiteman Knowledge," in *Manlike Monsters on Trial: Early Records and Modern Evidence*, ed. Marjorie Halpin and Michael M. Ames (Vancouver: UBC Press, 1980), 111; and James B. Waldram, *Revenge of the Windigo: The Construction of the Mind and Mental Health of North American Aboriginal Peoples* (Toronto: University of Toronto Press, 2004), 5, 192–5, and 205–11.

Cree, Anishinabek, Dunne-za, and Innu peoples.[31] While he focuses primarily on the correlation between *wetiko* belief and behaviour, to argue for the existence of a culturally bound psychotic disorder (windigo psychosis) that involved obsessing about or actually eating human flesh,[32] he does acknowledge that a wide variety of psychiatric symptoms seemed to be united by the *wetiko* theme.[33] He argues, "The Windigo is perceived within the culture as deviant from its norms. He is seen as a clear and severe case of psycho-social dysfunctioning."[34]

Teicher does provides some interesting insights about taboo behaviours in any culture, but unfortunately he remains bounded by the prevailing stereotypical assumptions about Indigenous people that pervade most academic accounts. For example, while it is a valid insight that beliefs (such as the possibility that someone could turn into a *wetiko*) affect the interpretation of events and suggest a range of appropriate responses, Teicher sees these patterns as "rigidly held," leaving "no room for alternatives." Discussing a *wetiko* execution, he argues, "Unlike a more complex culture, holding multi-causational and transactional notions of behaviors, the belief system in this situation dictated the one-cause explanation and the one-path action."[35] This is a startling conclusion, given the complexity revealed within Teicher's own compilation of *wetiko* accounts.

While execution of the *wetiko* was an option for action, it was rarely the first one attempted, let alone "inevitable."[36] Teicher himself points out that in his study, only in less than half the cases (thirty-three) was the individual who had become or was becoming a *wetiko* killed. Of the remaining thirty-seven cases, ten individuals recovered, nine were ostracized, two were eaten themselves, and one committed suicide.[37]

---

31 Teicher, "Windigo Psychosis," 7.

32 Ibid., 7.

33 Ibid., 112.

34 Ibid., 5.

35 Ibid., 78.

36 Ibid., 81, explaining another case, states, "Death, with the burning of the body, was inevitable." This is especially peculiar, given the fact the account itself describes a period of *three years*, where Wiskahoo expressed Windigo desires, *which did not last long* when drinking, and was simply tied up slightly until this passed. It was only three years afterwards that "this sad mood came upon him so often the natives got alarmed." Then "they" shot him.

37 Ibid., 108. In fifteen cases, the final outcome was unknown.

This complexity militates against the simplistic conclusion that all the *wetiko* accounts reveal a one-cause explanation and one-path action. Rather, the accounts gathered by Teicher himself reveal there was a variety of responses to and outcomes concerning this urgent issue. Logically, this suggests groups and individual agents must have made pragmatic assessments of particular situations (Is this person becoming or already a *wetiko*?) and normative decisions about which response was appropriate, given the particular situation (If yes, then how is this dangerous condition best responded to?).

Lou Marano, in his seminal article on the subject, flatly rejects and likely proves that there is not sufficient recorded behavioural evidence to justify the existence of a "windigo psychosis" from an anthropological or psychiatric point of view.[38] He suggests that more focus should be given to "group socio-dynamics rather than individual psychodynamics"[39] but concludes this promising line of inquiry with the unsatisfying argument that *all* recorded accounts of *wetiko* executions were "a rather predictable – though culturally conditioned – variant of triage homicide and witch hunting typical of societies under stress."[40] As part of what he sees as proof of this conclusion, he discusses the inclusive nature of Indigenous use of the *wetiko* concept. After a thorough review of the literature on a "windigo psychosis," he concludes, "The works of Saindon, Landes, Honigmann, Ridington ... and Preston ... all indicate in different ways that 'windigo' is a much more inclusive mental and phenomenological category for Northern Algonkians than the cannibal-psychotic of anthropological renown."[41] He sees this conclusion as being confirmed and amplified by his own field experiences, where he had never heard "windigo" associated with cannibalism and aggression.[42]

Marano does not go so far as to deny the existence and active use of a *wetiko concept* in the 1970s within northern Anishinabek societies, and in fact, he provides three examples of *wetiko* stories told to him during his five years residing in the community. One story involved a young man who disappeared after being angry at his mother for not returning home when he expected her. He was found only years later. The second story concerned a middle-aged woman who disappeared into the forest and

---

38 Marano et al., "Windigo Psychosis," 385.
39 Ibid.
40 Ibid.
41 Ibid., 392.
42 Ibid.

was found "barefoot and disheveled" after receiving news her youngest son had been killed. The third case involved a girl who was lost in the bush for three days before being found, barely recognizable, by her father. Marano himself witnessed an incident in which a young woman feared she was "becoming windigo" during a severe bout of postpartum depression.[43] He acknowledges, "Conditions and concepts change over time,"[44] and he explains his understanding, presumably based on the above stories, that "almost turning into a windigo" meant something very close to "being driven to distraction"; "being overcome with grief"; " being out of one's mind with worry"; and "being at one's wit's end." Finally, he concurs with Preston's speculation that *wetiko* scares "are often related to the mystery and great concern over lost persons."[45]

Following Marano's article, academic discussion of the *wetiko* concept diverged in two different directions. On the one hand, some writers have built on Marano's effective dismantlement of an empirical evidentiary basis for a culturally bound "windigo psychosis" to argue that *wetiko* ideation and behaviour never actually existed, and instead, that contemporary Indigenous people themselves see these stories only as myths.[46] On the other hand, Robert Brightman responded by distinguishing between a "windigo psychosis," created by academics, and a "windigo disorder" that is indigenous to and makes sense within an Algonquian context and cosmology.

---

43 Ibid., 387.

44 Ibid., 392.

45 Ibid., 386. Unfortunately for us, rather than exploring how the *wetiko* concept may have changed over time, how different factual situations might result in different societal responses, or how societal processes that result in sanction or death can potentially be manipulated for the gain, or to protect the misdeeds, of evil people, Marano concludes that *all* recorded accounts of executions of accused *wetikos* were triage homicide or witch hunts.

46 See Waldram, *Revenge of the Windigo*, 192–5. Waldram begins his book by reporting a conversation he had over a campfire where he was "patronizingly" informed, "It's just a story" when questioning the windigo's reality. While he had heard "time and again the stories of the windigo (or wetiko)" during his "considerable time in Algonquian communities in northern Canada," he reports "the Cree and Ojibwa I encountered did not seem overly concerned with the question of the windigo's reality" (5). See also the comment on Marino's paper by M. Jean Black: "After 18 years, on and off, of fieldwork in the eastern Subartic I had not myself found anything more than a general belief in windigo and occasional rumors of something more. Perhaps I was looking for what I thought I should find rather than what was there." Marano et al., "Windigo Psychosis," 398.

Brightman argues against reducing *wetiko* beliefs into "figments of ethnological imagination" or "as reducible to their purported functional effects" and argues Marano oversimplifies and distorts what is a "vastly more differentiated and recondite array of conceptions."[47] First, he reviews the different linguistic roots of the *wetiko* concept in Eastern Algonquian, Montagnais, Cree, and Ojibwa-Saulteaux to argue the concept was clearly present, at least from early in the contact period.[48] Second, he carefully reviews several second-hand accounts and ethnographic summaries that indicate that the majority of recorded *wetiko* cases demonstrate the conventional response was a cure rather than execution.[49] Brightman thus casts doubt on Marano's witch-hunt book, and also reveals the insufficiency of his witch-hunt argument "relative to the complexity of its object."[50]

Brightman goes on to discuss his understanding of a *wetiko* disorder as an open-ended, dynamic, and variable cultural complex that makes sense within a Northern Algonquian structural ideology,[51] which included certain understandings of the influential effects of famine cannibalism,[52] possession,[53] and dreaming and visions.[54] While Brightman's book takes us further in the logical direction I suggest and is certainly more thoughtful and respectful than Marano's or Teicher's, his ultimate conclusion does not help us in our inquiry much more than Teicher's does.[55] He argues the "windigo ideology created cannibalism by convincing some individuals they were predestined to it," and that the cure and execution of such individuals "re-created, validated, and modified the premises of the windigo ideology and the structural categories that

---

47 Brightman, "Windigo in the Material World," 338.
48 Ibid., 344.
49 Ibid., 358.
50 Ibid., 361.
51 Ibid., 363. Robin Ridington's comparison between the "wechuge" and the "windigo" concepts in Athapaskan and Algonquin societies is a similar attempt to place these concepts within a broader conceptual context. See, generally, Robin Ridington, "Wechuge and Windigo: A Comparison of Cannibal Belief among Boreal Forest Athapaskans and Algonquians," in *Little Bit Know Something: Stories in the Language of Anthropology*, 107–29 (Vancouver: Douglas and McIntyre, 1990).
52 Brightman, "Windigo in the Material World," 364.
53 Ibid., 366.
54 Ibid., 366–7.
55 Ibid., 374.

organized it." After all, he simply posits a self-perpetuating cycle of socially held beliefs and behaviours.

What is more important for our purposes is Brightman's final comment. He concludes his article by arguing there has been a historical transformation of the *wetiko* concept that "remains to be addressed":

> The passing of the itinerant winter round and the inception of micro-urban reservation communities have been accompanied or preceded by the passing of windigo cannibalism and windigo executions … Christianity, Euro-Canadian judicial institutions, and the elimination of famine (in calorific if not nutritional terms) are certainly implicated. Only metaphorically, as with the transferred usages "violent person" or "murderer," does the windigo today acquire known human denotata. The windigo of the 1980s, as I have learned of it in Cree communities in northern Manitoba, is a monster of human but otherwise unknown antecedency, a spiritually empowered cannibal that dwells in the bush entirely outside the trapline camps and settlements upon which it continues intermittently to impinge.[56]

This is an important point, because both Marano and Brightman acknowledge that, in their personal experiences among different groups of Cree and Anishinabek people in the 1970s and 1980s, the *wetiko* concept was still salient within these particular communities, although they were not aware of it being used to describe actual people obsessing about or engaging in *cannibalistic* ideation and behaviour in those communities at that time. Teicher, Marano, and Brightman, in different ways and for different purposes, all illustrate the diversity and complexity of the *wetiko* concept through time.

The information generously shared by Cree elders and other community members in interviews for this project confirms the continued salience and complexity of, as well as possible transformations of behaviours associated with, the *wetiko* concept, for at least some Indigenous communities in 2009. While I was told several funny or eerie cannibal *wetiko* stories from the long past, two elders said those stories come from their parents' time or before. One elder said that, while her father used to say hearing a *wetiko* yell from far away was quite common, especially during one winter, it rarely happened anymore. She also noted that it was very rare now to see someone becoming a *wetiko* eating away their

---

56 Ibid.

lips and other flesh, a frequently described symptom in the literature and older oral stories. These changes were described to me reflectively and unsolicited. She also postulated possible reasons why these changes might have occurred.[57] Two elders described a *wetiko* as bad "spirits" inside a person.[58] Their young adult grandson shared his understanding that a *wetiko* was a "lost soul who preys on other lost souls."[59]

Two elders I interviewed still practise traditional medicine, and one talked matter-of-factly about two different situations in which she and her husband were called to help or heal someone who was becoming a *wetiko*. In the first, a terrified mother phoned them for help because her daughter "was acting strange" and would sleep with a butcher knife under her pillow at night. In later years, this woman did seem to exhibit more predatory-like behaviours, apparently looking "hungrily" at people, "licking her lips." In the second, a man was brought in from another community for help because he was experiencing dissociative states and couldn't remember fights the next day or even that he had been beaten up. Finally, when we were talking about a sad incident involving a distant relative who was addicted to drugs and had been trying to get her teenage daughter out of care just to use her for prostitution, the elder asked me if I thought that might also be "that."[60] This demonstrates a broad range of uses of the term within a contemporary context – and this by just one individual, albeit a very knowledgeable and thoughtful one.

---

57 The elder speculated that the change in frequency of the *wetiko* yells might be because it was so much colder in the past. As for the chewing away of lips, she thinks this particular behaviour likely indicated a curse, and it may be rarer because there is less bad medicine and more protection from it, now that so many people have converted to Christianity (she is Catholic *and* practises traditional medicine). See Interview 1.

58 Ibid. The spiritual aspect of the wetiko concept was unavoidable in every interview. I will discuss this later on.

59 Interview 5: Interview of anonymous community member, 14 June 2009, Alberta. According to their grandson, people in his grandparent's generation still believed in the *wetiko*, people in his mother's generation were ambivalent or unsure, and most people in his generation see it as superstition. His partner, who grew up on a southern reserve close to an urban centre, had never heard of the *wetiko* at all until our conversation.

60 Interview 1. The elder actually said the word "wetiko" once, and then simply said "that" or "that thing." She believes that talking about the *wetiko* might make one come. At this point, I asked if we should stop the interview, but two of her children, who were also present, did not believe this and saw it as more important to know the information for responding to *wetiko*s, so kept asking her questions. She continued to talk for some time.

Taken together, the academic literature and the information from the interviews suggests that the academic preoccupation with proving, disproving, or definitively explaining the existence of a *wetiko* disorder has missed the most obvious and interesting point that even their own data suggest: there is a much simpler explanation of broad, contested, and variable definitions of the *wetiko* concept by individuals, and within and between groups, as well as its likely transformation over generations and in changing contexts. That is, the *wetiko* concept is, in fact, likely best understood as a complex social concept with a history, much like terms like *law* or *citizenship*. Both Joseph Raz (law) and James Tully (citizenship) argue that such concepts are "what Wittgenstein called 'family resemblance' concepts."[61] Rather than one essential feature that is common to each meaning, there are "overlapping similarities and dissimilarities among their varied uses."[62] This means their meaning is dependent on context[63] and their use is "always open to contestation and reasoned disagreement" as well as being in "an endless process of continuity and innovation."[64] Understood in this light, there is nothing particularly suspect about varied or inventive uses of the term *wetiko* in varied contexts.[65] In fact, continued inventiveness and contestation attest to its enduring usefulness and applicability as an intellectual concept.[66] Given this, theorists who seek to explain all its uses through one essential definition or social purpose are bound to fail.[67]

---

61 Joseph Raz, "Can There Be a Theory of Law?" in *The Blackwell Guide to the Philosophy of Law and Legal Theory*, ed. Martin P. Golding and William A. Edmondson (Oxford: Blackwell Publishing, 2005), 330 [Raz]; and James Tully, "Two Meanings of Global Citizenship: Modern and Diverse" (presented at The Meanings of Global Citizenship Conference, 9–10 September 2005), 1. http://webcache.googleusercontent. com/search?q=cache:R4YtQgWaQS0J:www.law.uvic.ca/demcon/documents/ Tully%2520Presem%2520-%2520Two%2520Meanings%2520of%2520Global%2520 Citizenship%2520II.doc+&cd=1&hl=en&ct=clnk&gl=ca.

62 Tully, "Two Meanings of Global Citizenship," 1.

63 Raz, "Can There Be a Theory of Law?" 330.

64 Tully, "Two Meanings, of Global Citizenship," 1.

65 This seems to be Marino's assumption about the *wetiko* incidents he heard about and witnessed that did not involve cannibalism. However, he seems to ignore or dismiss the continued salience of the concept to the people telling him the stories and dealing with the difficult situations at hand.

66 Some Indigenous writers have used the *wetiko* concept as a device for passing normative judgment on Western imperialism, greed, and violence. See Basil Johnston, *The Manitous: The Supernatural World of the Ojibwa* (Toronto: Key Porter Books, 1995), 235–7; and Forbes, *Columbus and Other Cannibals*, 42.

67 Myself included. See below, chapter 3.

Arguing that the *wetiko* is best understood as a complex intellectual concept with a social and legal history is not to say it originated as an academic construct. It obviously did not. While concept formation may be considered "the heart of all social science research,"[68] not all concepts are developed by academics. For example, Raz argues that a crucial difference between explaining law and other social institutions is that the notion of law is not purely, or even originally, a concept developed by academics to "help with explaining some social phenomena." Rather, "it is a concept entrenched in our society's self-understanding. It is a common concept in our society and one which is not the preserve of any specialized discipline."[69] This in no way diminishes law. Nor does it diminish theorists' ability to interrogate law as an intellectual concept in order to gain greater clarity and understanding about historical and existing practices. Similarly, the fact that the *wetiko* is not a concept developed by academics, and may be a common concept entrenched in Cree and Anishinabek societal self-understandings, does not mean we cannot interrogate it to gain greater understanding about principles and practices associated with it.

While a complex, family resemblance concept like *wetiko* is impossible to definitively or permanently define as one thing or another, it is still necessary, for analytical clarity, to have some working definition for our analysis.[70] John Gerring suggests it is useful to identify a general definition and a contextual definition (a "definition-in-use") for a complex concept such as the *wetiko*.[71] One way of coming to a general definition from the various manifestations we have seen is to identify both an "ideal type"[72] and a minimal definition[73] of the *wetiko* concept.[74] In the case of the *wetiko*, the "ideal type" definition is likely related to the self- and other-consuming cannibal of lore. However, once we consider the range of behaviours described as *wetiko* or going *wetiko*, including cannibalism or cannibalistic ideation, as well as the other uses of the term, in scenarios that include distressed and erratic behaviours, self-harm, and threats, as

---

68 See John Gerring, *Social Sciences Methodology: A Criterial Framework* (New York: Cambridge University Press, 2001), 35.

69 Raz, "Can There Be a Theory of Law?" 331.

70 See Gerring, *Social Sciences Methodology*, 65–8.

71 Ibid., 69.

72 According to Gerring, an ideal type definition is defined as "those attributes that define a term in its purest, most 'ideal' form." Ibid., 71.

73 A minimum definition is defined as "those few attributes that all nonidiosyncratic uses of the term have in common." Ibid.

74 Gerring describes this process in ibid., 71–81.

well as murder and preying on or using others for one's own ends, the one common theme emerges. The major theme that the *wetiko* concept appears to connote across time, space, and changing contexts is *people who are already or are becoming harmful or destructive to themselves and/or others in socially taboo ways.*[75] This definition captures both cannibalism and people who disappear alone into the forest or plan to prostitute their daughters. There are potentially horrifying consequences of any of these behaviours.

The *Wetiko* as a Legal Concept

A contextual definition from the general definition of the *wetiko* concept depends, unsurprisingly, on the "particular problem, region, time-period and method" the concept is being used to help understand or interrogate.[76] I am using a legal method of analysis, based on my common-law training, to extract principles from *wetiko* stories and accounts that might be useful for the contemporary problem of lateral violence and child sexual victimization in Indigenous communities. While I am aware there are other contexts, including spiritual[77] or psychological,[78] in which a different contextual definition might be more appropriate, I believe it

---

75 Interestingly enough, Teicher, "Windigo Psychosis," 113, actually suggests that an area of research to be followed up after his study would "involve thematic analysis of content for a large number of mentally ill persons in our society, without regard to their specific psychiatric diagnosis," and that taboo behaviour could "provide a theme analogous to that of cannibalism among the Northeastern Indians" (he gives the examples of murder, incest, and abortion). This reflexive return to his familiar society to look at not only taboo, but dangerous and harmful behaviours, has not, to my knowledge, been followed up. Of course, it could be easily done now by simply following a line of *legal* cases about a particular offence.

76 Gerring, *Social Sciences Methodology*, 85.

77 It is clear from my interviews that, in becoming a *wetiko*, some people are still attended to, healed, and prayed for by traditional medicine people (Interview 1). While I will discuss my understandings of these processes as legal, with transferable principles, later on in this section, it is clear the working definition among medicine people may be very different from the one given here.

78 A predominant explanation of the *wetiko* concept, beyond the windigo psychosis, is that it is actually a way of describing a wide variety of mental illnesses. See Marano et al., "Windigo Psychosis," 389, citing Ruth Landes, "The Abnormal among the Ojibwa Indians," *Journal of Abnormal and Social Psychology* 33 (1938): 30; and Landes, "The Personality of the Ojibwa," *Journal of Personality* 6, no. 1 (1937): 46. Forbes and Borrows also make this suggestion: see Forbes, *Columbus and Other Cannibals*, 38 (calling it a disease); and John Borrows, *Canada's Indigenous Constitution* (Toronto: University of Toronto Press, 2010), 115 (saying the man executed as a *wetiko* was probably suffering from psychological illness).

makes the most sense for my inquiry to view the *wetiko* as a *legal* concept within (at least) broader Cree and Anishinabek legal traditions.

Beyond contextual and methodological convenience, there are at least three reasons it makes sense to view the *wetiko* as a legal concept. First, the subject matter is equivalent to any minimum content requirement necessary for a functioning legal order. Second, most accounts demonstrate a collective reasoning and problem-solving process. Third, in most accounts, the characterization of someone as a *wetiko* triggers felt obligations. Let me elaborate briefly on each of these points.

First, the subject matter of the *wetiko* concept: the need to address the unavoidable reality of human destructiveness and human vulnerability fits squarely within what is widely accepted as a vital part of the minimal content of any functional legal or moral order.[79] No one seriously argues against H.L.A. Hart's assertion that our human vulnerability means that one of "the most characteristic provision[s]" of any system of law or morals must include the prohibition or restriction of "violence in killing or inflicting bodily harm." While Hart does not argue that people are never altruistic, he does contend that the "tendencies to aggression are frequent enough to be fatal to social life if not controlled."[80]

Because some people can become harmful or destructive to others, and because we are vulnerable beings,[81] Hart is right to ask, "If there were not these rules then what point could there be for beings such as ourselves in having rules of *any* other kind?"[82] In fact, he argues that to ignore this aspect of human existence would be akin to the social arrangements of "a suicide club."[83] In absolutely no *wetiko* stories – either in the more mythological ones about giant *wetiko*s, or in the ones where a human transforms into one – is the *wetiko* allowed to endlessly prey on the vulnerable. Intervention to prevent *wetiko*

---

79 H.L.A. Hart, *The Concept of Law*, 2nd ed. (New York: Oxford University Press, 1994), 194.
80 Ibid., 196.
81 F.C. DeCoste, Review of *Law After Auschwitz*, by David Fraser, *Kings Law Journal* 18 (2007): 186–7: "We are law-needy beings because we are vulnerable beings ... We turn to law to save us safe from harm until our destiny calls us, each and every one of us in our turn."
82 Hart, *Concept of Law*, 192.
83 Ibid.

transformations and behaviours is *the* most consistent normative principle in these stories.[84]

Second, most *wetiko* accounts demonstrate a collective reasoning and practical problem-solving process that is distinctively legal. Gerald Postema has highlighted two crucial aspects of what common-law jurists call the "artificial reason" of law. First, legal reasoning is "the product of reflective practical experience."[85] Second, this "deliberative activity is never solitary, never done for one's own part only. The artificial reason of the law is common reason."[86] Thus, the "learned capacity for reflective judgment ... is a social capacity: the ability to reason from a body of shared experiences with normative significance to solutions for new practical problems. It is to judge what one has good reason to believe others in the community would regard as reasonable and fitting."[87]

Legal reasoning requires "a distinctive deliberative and discursive capacity ... an ability to articulate and defend judgments publicly."[88] Because legal judgments are public and collectively owned, they must be made in a way that elicits "recognition and acceptance as appropriate in one's community."[89]

As we shall see, while responses to a *wetiko* categorization vary considerably, it is clear that drastic decisions about necessary responses to a *wetiko* were almost always decided through a public, deliberative process. In some cases, individual responses to someone becoming a *wetiko* were also considered and judged as part of the same process. In all historical cases of *wetiko* executions within the Canadian court system, there is evidence the community involved recognized and accepted the decision to execute the *wetiko* as reasonable and appropriate under the factual circumstances.

Third, another predominant theme in almost every story and account is that the identification of an individual as a real or suspected *wetiko* triggers identifiable and *felt* obligations by others around him or her.

---

84 I will discuss this at greater length below, but the citations would be too endless to add in a footnote, because in almost *every* story the *wetiko* is eventually stopped from preying on others.

85 Gerald Postema, "Classical Common Law Jurisprudence, Part II," *Oxford Commonwealth Law Journal* 3 (2003): 10.

86 Ibid., 9.

87 Ibid.

88 Ibid., 16.

89 Ibid., 10.

Two perpetual questions for legal theorists, especially in regard to legal orders where there is no central source of authority, are what makes law *law*, as opposed to brute force or other forms of social normativity, and what makes law *binding*, aside from centralized enforcement mechanisms. In their recent treatise on international law, Jutta Brunnée and Stephen Toope argue, "The distinctiveness of law lies not in form or in enforcement but in the creation and effects of legal obligation."[90] From this perspective, legal obligation is "best viewed as an internalized commitment and not as an externally imposed duty matched with a sanction for non-performance."[91] In other words, the essence of law is a felt obligation to reason through its principles in one's affairs.[92] As we shall see, while recorded accounts of *wetiko* incidents rarely identify the reasoning processes of the Indigenous participants, patterns of behaviour as well as information from court transcripts and the interviews strongly suggest a remarkable consistency in people acting on felt obligations when someone was characterized as a *wetiko*.

Because of the context of my inquiry, and because the *wetiko* concept is employed in such distinctively legal ways, I argue that it is a legal concept integral to the legal traditions of some Indigenous societies. Thus, for the purposes of this inquiry, we will revise our minimal definition of the *wetiko* concept slightly for our working definition: the *wetiko* as *a legal categorization* describes people who are harmful or destructive to themselves and/or others in socially taboo ways.

---

90 Jutta Brunnée and Stephen Toope, "An Interactional Theory of International Legal Obligation," University of Toronto Faculty of Law, Legal Research Series no. 08-16, 2008, 3. https://papers.ssrn.com/sol3/papers.cfm?abstract_id=1162882.

91 Ibid., 17.

92 The obligation must be to "reason through" law, because Brunnée and Toope argue that "law can be distinguished from other forms of social normativity by the specific type of rationality apparent in the internal processes that make law possible. This rationality is dependent upon reasoned argument, reference to past practice and contemporary social aspirations, and the deployment of analogy. When the [Fuller's] eight criteria of legality are met, and when this particular rationality is evident, law will tend to attract its own adherence" (ibid., 17). For a compelling argument that Fuller's criteria for the internal morality of law depend on a view of subjects as agents, and thus the "removal of self-directed agency" (124) is incompatible with "law," see Kristen Rundle, "The Impossibility of an Exterminatory Legality: Law and the Holocaust," *University of Toronto Law Journal* 59 (2009): 486–504.

If we look at the *wetiko* concept as a legal category, it becomes even clearer why people who are familiar with it would use it to describe a relatively diverse set of observable behaviours. The idea of one legal category encompassing a broad range of harmful behaviours should not be terribly hard to understand for anyone who has researched the contemporary Western legal concept of "sex offender."[93] There is clearly a range of offending behaviours, and a range of offenders, but this does not detract from our belief that the term represents a real phenomenon. Police and other professionals use the term *sex offender* to describe both a teenager who exposes himself to younger children[94] and a serial sex offender who rapes his victims before beating them to death.[95] There are many variations and gradations between these two examples of dangerous, harmful, and taboo behaviours.[96] In addition, the concept changes over time. For example, the Canadian *Criminal Code* now contains the offence of "luring a child," which requires the use of the Internet.[97] Obviously, this behavioural manifestation of a sexual offence could not have even existed fifty years ago. There is

---

93 In their well-respected book, Perry and Orchard define a sexual offender as someone who "engages in sexual behaviour deemed by society to be inappropriate." Garry P. Perry and Janet Orchard, *Assessment and Treatment of Adolescent Sex Offenders* (Sarasota, FL: Professional Resource, 1992), 5.

94 See the inclusion of exhibitionism in a list of sexual offences described in ibid., 5.

95 For a *Globe and Mail* investigative piece using of the term *serial sex offender* to describe two Alberta men accused of murdering at least two women after brutally raping them, see Mathew McClearn and Kathryn Blaze Baum, "The Taken: Who Qualifies as a Serial Killer and More on Data behind the Project," https://beta.theglobeandmail.com/news/national/the-taken-who-qualifies-as-a-serial-killer-and-more-on-the-data-behind-the-project/article27443307/?ref=http://www.theglobeandmail.com&. The well-known Robert Pickton case is another recent obvious example of this extreme.

96 There are numerous sexual offences described in the Canadian *Criminal Code*, including, but not limited to sexual interference (s. 151), invitation to sexual touching (s. 152), sexual exploitation (s. 153), incest (s. 155), anal intercourse (s. 159), bestiality (s. 160), making or distributing child pornography (s. 163.1), parent or guardian procuring sexual activity (s. 170), and luring a child (s. 172.1). Edward L. Greenspan and Marc Rosenberg, ann., *Martin's Annual Criminal Code 2006* (Aurora, ON: Canada Law Book, 2006). Perry and Orchard, *Assessment and Treatment of Adolescent Sex Offenders*, 5, describe the terms *sexual offences* as including "both coercive or noncoercive sexual acts, including oral and vaginal penetration (by penis, hand or other objects) or sexual touching or fondling, and so-called hands-off offences such as exhibitionism, voyeurism, and obscene telephone calls."

97 *Criminal Code*, RSC 1985, c C-46, as amended, s. 172.1.

no logical reason to think the *wetiko* concept could not have similar breadth and fluidity over time, and substantial evidence that shows that it did (and does).

Looking Again at the *Wetiko* Stories: A Present-Tense, Trans-Systemic Approach to Legal Obligations, Principles, and Processes

The *wetiko* is a legal concept – a legal categorization that triggered (or triggers) collective reasoning processes and felt obligations within broader Indigenous legal traditions. From a legal perspective, the major question in approaching the range of *wetiko* incidents (or sexual offences) does not lie in redefining, dismissing, or definitively explaining one manifestation or another. Rather, it lies in identifying particular obligations, legitimate collective reasoning processes, and legal principles for determining an appropriate response in particular circumstances. Unfortunately, very little legal or scholarly attention has been paid to *how* Cree and Anishinabek people collectively assessed (or assess) the threat posed by people who fit within the *wetiko* category, and what the range of obligations and appropriate societal responses were (or are) based on that assessment.

There is very little legal scholarship in this area, and only one recorded common-law case.[98] Sydney Harring provides a thorough review and insightful analysis of the Canadian common-law treatment of "wendigo killers" in the late nineteenth and early twentieth century, pointing out these reveal both legal imperialism and the intactness of traditional Indigenous law at that time.[99] He argues the *wetiko* "mythology" was incorporated into a "well-established ... traditional legal order, inseparable from religion"[100] in Cree, Saulteaux, and Ojibway societies. These traditional legal orders "provided mechanisms designed to let small hunting bands make difficult legal decisions involving life and death."[101]

---

98 *R v Machekequonabe* [1897] OJ No 98, 2 CCC 138.
99 Sidney L. Harring, "The Enforcement of the Extreme Penalty: Canadian Law and the Ojibwa-Cree Spirit World," in *White Man's Law: Native People in Nineteenth-Century Canadian Jurisprudence*, ed. Sidney L. Harring (Toronto: University of Toronto Press, 1998), 217. See also the excerpt from Fiddler and Stevens, *Killing the Shaman* in a criminal law case book: Jennie Abell and Elizabeth Sheehy, *Criminal Law and Procedure: Cases, Context and Critique*, 3rd ed. (Concord ON: Captus, 2002), 53.
100 Harring, "Enforcement of the Extreme Penalty," 219.
101 Ibid., 237.

At the same time, when an execution took place, and Indigenous people were tried before Canadian courts, these Indigenous legal orders were not recognized as legal orders. In fact, as Harring points out, this seemed to be part of an explicit policy intended to extend the power of Canadian law over Indigenous peoples.[102] In this way, Indigenous law was reduced to "pagan belief,"[103] "superstitious belief," or "a form of insanity to which the whole tribe is subjected."[104] On these terms, neither a "reasonable exercise of self-defence"[105] nor "ignorance of the law" held up as defences.[106] As stated by the judge in the Fiddler case, "What the law forbids, no pagan belief can justify."[107] In another case, the federal government arranged for a commutation of a death sentence on policy grounds by arguing that judging "the conduct of a savage governed by superstitious belief and whose habits are entirely opposed to civilization" might interfere with the civilizing project by creating the impression "contact with civilization imperiled their existence."[108] They argued Indigenous people should be treated by the law as "a child below the age of fourteen years."[109]

There are two points worth making about Harring's explanation of the *wetiko* itself. First, his description of the *wetiko* concept focuses on the "ideal type" definition above, complete with its supernatural qualities and spiritual beliefs.[110] As we have seen, this is not a sufficient definition, and care must be taken to avoid distortions that might result from this conceptual insufficiency.[111] Second, understandably, because of his

---

102 Ibid., 235.

103 Ibid., 232.

104 Ibid., 223.

105 Ibid., 224 and 227.

106 Ibid., 217, saying *R v Machekeqoonabe* is "one of the best known indigenous law cases in the common law world, often cited for the proposition that the criminal law universally applies even when the indigenous peoples involved had never been exposed to the common law and were completely ignorant of it."

107 Ibid., 232.

108 Ibid., 235.

109 Ibid., 236. Thus, there should be "a prima facie presumption that he does not understand the nature and consequences of his act."

110 Ibid., 218–19.

111 Particularly, my concern is that an overemphasis on the spiritual aspects and supernatural qualities told about a *wetiko* can lead us to focus on the "honestly held" *belief* in the *wetiko*, rather than the legitimacy of the legal processes to address someone suspected of being or becoming a *wetiko*. For example, even if we accept the spiritual premises in the Fiddler case (where the woman had not yet become a *wetiko*) as a starting point, it still raises the difficult issue of whether or when the use of pre-emptive force within a legal order is acceptable.

focus, Harring addresses only historical *wetiko* accounts that ended in executions. This creates its own distortions, because execution was such a rare response historically[112] and because people on trial for their lives have very good reason to lie about exactly what happened.[113] It also means Harring speculates unnecessarily about possible "hidden" *wetiko* killings in other homicide cases,[114] which could inadvertently reinforce the misperception that the characterization of someone as a *wetiko* always led to his or her death.

These cautions aside, Harring's work is very useful, for his thorough research of *Wetiko* cases in Canadian law, and his demonstration that these cases were united and grounded in a policy of crushing Indigenous sovereignty. As well, the fact that a complete dismissal of both collective reasoning processes and individual mental capacity reached the level of law and resulted in deaths and imprisonment is a good demonstration of how beliefs affected judicial and government behaviour within nineteenth- and early twentieth-century Canadian society. Cultural beliefs about Indigenous people (as savages, superstitious, childlike) "dictated the one-cause explanation and the one-path action" of murder convictions in cases of *wetiko* executions.[115] This might help explain why so many theorists missed the obvious explanation that the *wetiko* was (and is) a complex intellectual concept that forms an integral part of some Indigenous legal traditions.

John Borrows recognizes responses to a *wetiko* categorization as part of Indigenous legal traditions. His brief work on this topic is the most logically compelling and useful for approaching *wetiko* accounts and stories by employing a legal lens. Borrows explicates specific legal principles from one historical description of an Anishinabek account of a

---

112 Of course, as Borrows also stresses, executions *never* occur now. Borrows, *Canada's Indigenous Constitution*, 111–15.

113 Harring points this obvious point out, referring to the conflicting testimonies in *The Queen v Payoo and Napaysoosee* [Moostoos] case and the unlikely account of a witness being an unwitting participant in a strangling in the Fiddler case. See Harring, "Enforcement of the Extreme Penalty," 227 and 231.

114 Harring argues that other homicide cases demonstrate a careful distorting of the facts to hide the fact they were actually *wetiko* killings (217). This may have indeed been the case, but Harring does not give compelling reasons to accept this view. See Harring, "Enforcement of the Extreme Penalty," 224, and the case of Paul Sabourin, 234.

115 Teicher, *Windigo Psychosis*, 78 (of course, actually referring to Indigenous actions in *wetiko* executions). This is intended in fun. I am not an anthropologist and can claim no authority on the prevailing assumptions of another time.

process leading up to and following a *wetiko* execution.[116] He suggests both that contemporary Anishinabek people might find such principles familiar,[117] and that it is worth considering how the underlying legal principles might apply in the contemporary context.[118] Borrows also points out that "a vast literature shows this pattern of dealing over long periods of time, and in different geographic regions where the Anishinabek lived." While he stresses that such a process would never lead to killing the man in question today, he does argue "the underlying principles in this account remain."[119]

Before engaging with the specific principles Borrows lists, it is important to discuss *how* he goes about identifying them in the first place. Although Borrows does not explicitly discuss his methodology, three major, interrelated aspects of his approach have been very influential in my own analysis. First, Borrows's starting assumptions about Indigenous people in historical accounts as reasoning people within broader, reasonable legal traditions allows him to access the historical rationality of their actions. Second, his focus on the contemporary application of legal principles as present-tense intellectual resources contributes to the continuing health and vitality of living legal traditions. Third, his focus on the social responses to the universal human problem represented by the *wetiko* concept and his bracketing of the big questions about "supernatural" aspects (when practicable and non-distorting) increases present accessibility to these intellectual resources.

Starting Assumptions about the Past:
Reasoning People in Reasonable Legal Orders

When looking at the past, Borrows begins from the reasonable assumption that the Anishinabek people involved in the historical *wetiko* incident were not particularly stupid, superstitious, child-like,

---

116 As part of my information package for the interviews for this project, John Borrows generously allowed me to use this excerpt so interviewees would have an idea of the approach I am taking to the *wetiko* stories. Borrows, *Canada's Indigenous Constitution*, 115.

117 Ibid.

118 John Borrows and Leonard Rotman, *Aboriginal Legal Issues: Cases, Materials, and Commentary*, 2nd ed. (Toronto: LexisNexis Canada, 2003), 908–19.

119 Borrows, *Canada's Indigenous Constitution*, 114.

or crazy.[120] Nor does he assume they were acting out pathologically in response to broad social distress.[121] By assuming they were reasoning agents, acting in reasonable, principled ways, he is able to articulate principles from the historical description of their actions. This helps us to access the "historical rationality" that is so often lost when discussing "customary law."[122] In my analysis of *wetiko* cases, I adopt Borrows's starting assumptions about the likely reasonableness and intelligence of the Indigenous people whose actions are described in historical accounts.

Borrows also assumes these incidents were part of larger legal traditions.[123] As Val Napoleon has argued in the case of African customary law, it is reasonable to contextualize legal concepts such as the *wetiko* as one aspect of a "comprehensive whole," a broader, functioning Indigenous legal tradition "(1) that was large enough to avoid conflicts of interest and which ensured accountability, (2) that had collective processes to change law as necessary with changing times and changing norms, (3) that was able to deal with internal oppressions, (4) that was legitimate and the outcomes collectively owned, and (5) that had collective legal reasoning processes."[124]

These assumptions prevent an analysis that reduces the *wetiko* concept to a question of "honestly held beliefs"[125] or even rigidly adhered-to rules.[126]

---

120 For these legal views, see Harring, "Enforcement of the Extreme Penalty," starting at note 118.

121 Recall Marano's argument was that *wetiko* incidents were a symptom of "traumatized societies" in the nineteenth century. Marano et al., "Windigo Psychosis," 397.

122 H. Patrick Glenn, "The Capture, Reconstruction and Marginalization of 'Custom,'" *American Journal of Comparative Law* 45 (1997): 617. Glenn points out that when a custom is merely seen as repetitive behaviour, we cannot "penetrate the historical rationality of," it becomes "difficult if not impossible to justify; it must be constantly held up to the rigorous standards of present rationality" (613).

123 Borrows, *Canada's Indigenous Constitution*, 111.

124 Val Napoleon, "Ayook: Gitksan Legal Order, Law, and Legal Theory" (PhD diss., University of Victoria, Faculty of Law, 2009) 47–8. It is simply beyond the scope of this book to explore Cree or Anishinabek legal traditions as wholes. I acknowledge this limits the usefulness of *wetiko* legal principles, but am confident an increasing number of legal theorists are doing this important work.

125 Harring argues Canadian law could have accommodated Indigenous groups by "attempting to incorporate the honestly held beliefs of Indians into the traditional common law defences." See Harring, "Enforcement of the Extreme Penalty," 238.

126 Reducing law to simple rules, while missing or ignoring the necessary legal reasoning, perpetuates "the stereotypical myth that indigenous people had little or no intellectual life, but just followed rules and stoically upheld unchanging morals." See Napoleon, "Ayook," 29.

Rather they create the intellectual space for analysing historical *wetiko* incidents as one small part of larger complex and dynamic legal traditions, with collective reasoning processes and mechanisms for accountability and change.[127]

Such starting assumptions should not be confused with idealizing the past. Logical assumptions about the capacity of historic Indigenous individuals and legal traditions must include logical assumptions that human frailties also exist, and that all legal cultures are incomplete.[128] The health and usefulness of laws depend on our ability to "rigorously and critically examine them."[129] This includes recognizing internal power imbalances, and heeding the insight of de Sousa Santos that, for a true picture of any legal order, we must look, not only to the law, but also to the lawlessness that accompanies it.[130] Attending to these realities allows space for the necessary work of thinking "through the questions, contradictions and conflicts" within law.[131] My analysis of the *wetiko* stories and accounts assumes both that the actions described are principled and reasoned, and they are embedded in broader legal traditions. However, it also includes critical questions about these actions and traditions when they arise.

Focus on Contemporary Application of
Legal Principles as Present-Tense Intellectual Resources

Borrows focuses on *contemporary* application of the legal principles he explicates from a historical account. This is a distinctively legal approach to the past. Martin Krygier maintains that all law is best understood as "a profoundly traditional social practice."[132] Trans-systemic legal

---

127 Napoleon argues that, by focusing on a subjective belief in witchcraft in a South African murder case, rather than integrating customary law as a comprehensive whole, legal theorists "appear to assume that there was no way that African customary law could change with the times so that people could deal with today's witchcraft killings according to current social and legal norms, and politics" (ibid., 47).

128 Boaventura de Sousa Santos argues that all cultures are incomplete, and recognizing this is a necessary step in the work of translation between them. See Boaventura de Sousa Santos, *The World Social Forum: A User's Manual* (Coimbra: Centre for Social Studies 2004), 29. http://www.ces.uc.pt/bss/documentos/fsm_eng.pdf.

129 Val Napoleon, Angela Cameron, Colette Arcand, and Dahti Scott, "Where's the Law in Restorative Justice?" in *Aboriginal Self Government in Canada: Current Trends and Issues,* ed. Yale Belanger, 3rd ed. (Saskatoon, SK: Purich Publishing, 2008), 22.

130 Boaventura de Sousa Santos, "A Critique of Lazy Reason: Against the Waste of Experience" (paper presented to the DemCon Conference, 1 December 2006).

131 Napoleon, "Ayook," 312.

132 Martin Krygier, "Law as Tradition," *Law and Philosophy* 5, no. 2 (1986): 237.

theorists agree that understanding law as legal traditions, rather than self-contained systems, makes the most sense and is the best way for exploring it intellectually, rather than instrumentally.[133] Rod MacDonald and Jason MacLean argue that the "study of law is ... an interpretative practice"[134] and we should openly acknowledge it as such. In regard to the common-law tradition, Krygier points out that legal practitioners are "not engaged in disinterested forays into legal history." They tend to treat the past as if it were "a vast storehouse to be searched for solutions to present problems."[135] Krygier argues that, while this may look like bad history, it makes sense when viewed as "simply typical of the behaviour of participants in a tradition."[136] To learn about law is not to memorize rules or capture some authentic, authoritative moment, but to have "an open-ended conversation about law through time."[137]

Borrows has argued elsewhere that the recognition and affirmation of Indigenous peoples' physical and intellectual mobility is "crucial to future health of Indigenous peoples."[138] He writes, "We are not past-tense peoples. We should be physically free to travel through space and philosophically at liberty to carry our ideas through time."[139] This intellectual mobility in law is vital because, as Val Napoleon explains, if "legal traditions are determined to be incapable of change or are pinioned in the past, their theoretical and intellectual resources will no longer be available.[140] Both Borrows and Napoleon argue that if legal principles, processes, and obligations are going to be seen by both insiders and outsiders as part of living legal traditions, rather than as "cultural remnants," they must be seen as relevant in today's world[141] as well as

---

133 Roderick A. MacDonald and Jason MacLean, "Navigating the Transsystemic: No Toilets in the Park," *McGill Law Journal* 50 (2005): 721.
134 Ibid., 727.
135 Krygier, "Law as Tradition," 248.
136 Ibid., 249.
137 MacDonald and MacLean, "Navigating the Transsystemic," 737.
138 John Borrows, "Physical Philosophy: Mobility and the Future of Indigenous Rights," in *Indigenous Peoples and the Law: Comparative and Critical Perspectives*, ed. Benjamin J. Richardson, Shin Imai, and Kent McNeil (Portland, OR: Hart Publishing, 2009), 419.
139 Ibid.
140 Napoleon, "Ayook," 91.
141 Napoleon et al., "Where's the Law in Restorative Justice?" 21.

"useful in tackling contemporary concerns" and "current needs."[142] As Napoleon puts it, "Law is something people *do* … [so] if it is not practical and useful to life … why bother?"[143]

By looking at the legal past for its precedential value in the present, Borrows creates the necessary space for thinking creatively and actively through Indigenous legal norms *today*. His focus on contemporary application of legal principles increases the likelihood they will remain available as useful and usable intellectual resources that healthy societies can continue to draw on, adapt, and apply to ongoing circumstances.[144] In the analysis that follows, I will draw on historic and contemporary *wetiko* legal principles as intellectual resources that I argue may have the potential of being applied, as precedent or by analogy, to pressing contemporary issues of lateral violence and child sexual victimization. This is approached as an interpretative exercise, just one contribution to an ongoing conversation over time. However, I am undertaking it because I am hopeful it has potential to be useful and practical in real life today.

Universal Human Problems: Focusing on Social Processes instead of Individual Pathology, and Bracketing the Big Questions Where Practicable and Non-Distorting

Finally, in his work, Borrows focuses on the universal human problem the *wetiko* legal principles address, and the social processes for dealing with this, rather than on the individual pathology of the *wetiko* himself or herself[145] or on "big questions" about cosmological or supernatural aspects

---

142 John Borrows, *Recovering Canada: The Resurgence of Indigenous Law* (Toronto: University of Toronto Press, 2006), 147.

143 Napoleon, "Ayook," 312.

144 Bartlett points out that when a tradition "stops making sense under existing circumstances" it will not continue. This means "the strength of a tradition is not how closely it adheres to its original form but how well it is able to develop and remain relevant under changing circumstances." See Katharine T. Bartlett, "Tradition, Change, and the Idea of Progress in Feminist Legal Thought" (1995) *Wisconsin Law Review* 303 (1995): 330.

145 This was also Marano's refreshing change of focus, but he was unable to accomplish what Borrows has because of his above-noted assumptions about the group socio-dynamics being about social *pathology*. See Marano et al., "Windigo Psychosis," 385.

of the *wetiko* concept. This approach is particularly useful when dealing with *wetiko* accounts, because there has been so much academic speculation about these aspects. Refocusing on social responses and the universal aspect of the concept encourages the reader or listener to avoid "exoticizing" or over-particularizing the *wetiko*, and instead recognize the universal human problem, the "ordinariness of human monstrousness"[146] that the Anishinabek group was forced to face in the incident in question. How do we, as a group, respond when someone among us, whom we may know and love, becomes dangerous or threatens imminent harm? I agree wholeheartedly with Hannah Arendt that it is evil that is banal – be it cannibalism or concentration camps; we give it too much credit if we elevate it beyond an absence of thought, imagination, and judgment.[147] It is much more interesting to examine how we collectively respond, creatively, tragically, compassionately, resolutely, courageously to that absence among us. As Postema's work demonstrates, these collective reasoning processes are also the very stuff of law, and the most appropriate focus for a legal analysis of any given situation.

The fact that *wetiko* stories and accounts often involve "supernatural" aspects may partially explain why Euro-Canadian legal and academic writers often view them as explainable only in terms of beliefs, whether derisively or respectfully. Harring points out frankly that "traditional reasons for [*wetiko* killings] defied the moral sensibilities of Euro-Canadians. A world of evil spirits in the forest that would kill you if you did not kill them first made complete sense to Ojibwa and Cree Indians; it made no sense at all to whites."[148]

A remarkably similar point is made recently by Metis scholar Nathan Carlson, who concludes his extensive study of the *wetiko* concept by arguing, "The witiko phenomenon and condition, on the whole, has yet to be properly accounted for within a Western paradigm." He believes this is at least partially "the result of a reluctance to include Algonquian

---

146 Marano et al., "Windigo Psychosis," 401 (Ruth Landes's response).
147 See generally, Hannah Arendt, *Eichmann in Jerusalem: A Report on the Banality of Evil* (London: Faber and Faber, 1963). While Arendt focuses on administrative, political evil, we will see that the harm to other people as an absence of the human qualities of thought, judgment, and imagination resonates with many traditional multicausal explanations of why someone transforms into a *wetiko*. See particularly, Basil Johnston, *The Manitous: The Supernatural World of the Ojibway* (Toronto: Key Porter Books, 1995), 224; Interview 4.
148 Harring, "Enforcement of the Extreme Penalty," 238.

etiology" in the discussion, and suggests "the perspective of the northern Algonquians must inform any further consideration of the witiko phenomenon."[149]

Both these accounts posit a significant gap in the basic understandings of Euro-Canadians and Indigenous thinkers that prevents the *wetiko* concept from making sense within a Western paradigm. Yet Borrows has clearly managed to present the Anishinabek legal principles regarding the *wetiko* concept to a largely Western, legally trained audience. In the account he uses, the Anishinabek group recounts finding ice that will not melt when they burn the body. This does not seem possible from a Western perspective. How did he bridge such a gap?

Certainly, his starting assumptions of (1) reasoning people and traditions, his focus on (2) contemporary application of legal principles, and (3) on legitimate social reasoning processes, rather than individual pathology, help here. The detail of the ice simply does not make it into Borrows's analysis, but why should it? It is actually immaterial to the legal principles that could be applicable in a contemporary issue of imminent harm. Ice or no ice, burning a body is no longer a legal option.[150] Neither, of course, is execution, but, assuming the purpose of execution was removing or incapacitating someone when needed, there are still options, such as incarceration, for accomplishing this purpose. In this case, as long as one begins from Borrows's first assumption – that the group is not superstitious or crazy – the ice is not an obstacle to anyone sincerely wishing to access Anishinabek law today.[151] By bracketing this "supernatural" aspect of the story, Borrows makes the legal principles more accessible to a greater number of both Anishinabek and non-Anishinabek people, because his analysis does not turn or fall on immersion in the cosmology from which the *wetiko* concept emerges.[152]

---

149 Nathan D. Carlson, "Reviving Witiko (Windigo): An Ethnohistory of 'Cannibal Monsters' in the Athabasca District of Northern Alberta, 1878–1910," *Ethnohistory* 56, no. 3 (2009): 382.
150 Although if the person died of natural causes, the family could choose cremation.
151 The spiritual and supernatural aspects of the *wetiko* concept are unavoidable, and I will take this up later in this section.
152 Many Indigenous people today are not growing up, entirely, or at all, within the cosmology that Carlson argues is a crucial component to properly understanding the *wetiko* concept. Despite the comprehensive and detailed knowledge shared by elders, the younger people I interviewed knew very little about the principled response to the *wetiko* (see Interviews 4 and 5). This illustrates why it is so important to build a Cree legal pedagogy.

I do not mean to minimize the importance of understanding the broader cosmology of a legal tradition.[153] Ignoring these "foundational elements" used to "create meaning and social order" risks reaching conclusions based on descriptive accounts of law that are "superficial and distorted."[154] However, in the case of legal and academic treatment of the *wetiko* concept, the opposite is too often true – inexplicable "symptoms" or unfamiliar beliefs take centre stage, to the exclusion of any discussion about the equally obvious existence of principled action by reasoning agents. In the analysis that follows, I will follow Borrows in bracketing the bigger cosmological questions in the interests of accessibility to the legal principles.

Some "supernatural" signs and symptoms and "spiritual" means were discussed in my interviews for this project. Unlike the ice in Borrows's analysis, some of these are directly material to the legal principles and processes discussed. However, aside from generalities, older community members always spoke about these signs, symptoms, and means in a context of explaining their reasoned understandings about human agency, principled action, and response efficacy.[155] There was no good reason for them to lie to me,[156] but the reader or listener must accept my word about their sanity and intelligence. It *would* be distorting not to include these

---

153 Stavast points out that cosmologies and cultural views of the self form part of "the basic architecture of thought that social agents within a culture use in their legal reasoning and deliberation to determine the content of their laws and the shape of their legal orders." Kendall Stavast, "Cosmology, Self and Legal Order in Subarctic Athapaskan Society" (2008, author's collection), 1.

154 Ibid., 6–7.

155 Interviews 1, 2, and 4; Interview of anonymous community member, 13 June 2009, Alberta.

156 One elder, who did not know me well, stopped in the middle of a story that included a moose who sang a song and spoke to a man, to ask if I believed him. I tried to waffle, saying I wasn't there, but Carol, my translator, pushed me, asking, "Well, now you've heard the story, so do you believe it? Or do you think he is lying to you?" (Interview 2). This gentle confrontation forced me to think through what is often an implicit move in an explicit way. It is worthwhile considering the possibilities left to us when we prima facie dismiss the possibility the beliefs/accounts are true. Is the elder lying? Engaged in disingenuous lesson teaching? Or something more pernicious? Or is he or she mistaken? Naive? Unreasonable? Delusional? It is hard to come up with a respectful way of describing a person who claims something is true that we maintain is unquestionably false. See a similar point in Teicher, "Windigo Psychosis," 32, where the narrator says, "Grandma wouldn't tell me a lie – I don't think – but that's how I know her story is true."

"supernatural" elements in my legal analysis, so they will be included under the principles, for the purposes they were originally discussed. In this way, I hope my interpretation remains relevant and respectful to the community, while also being accessible to a broader audience.[157]

These three aspects of Borrows's methodology – (1) assuming reasoning agents in reasonable legal orders; (2) focusing on contemporary application of the legal principles; and (3) universalizing the human problem these principles address – help us to access the historic rationality, or logic, in descriptive accounts of law, approach the legal principles as useful parts of an ongoing conversation about law, and increase the accessibility of these principles. In the following chapters, I adopt this present-tense, trans-systemic methodology to proceed with a legal analysis of the *wetiko* accounts and stories in the literature and from the interviews.

---

157 I am not claiming it is authoritative, of course; it is just one interpretation, ideally at least useful fodder for critique and correction.

Chapter 3

Understanding the Dynamics: The *Wetiko* and Child Victimization – Tactics, Characteristics, and Possible Causes

In the previous chapter, I argued that the *wetiko* can be seen as a complex intellectual concept or legal category. While it has a wide range of uses and applications, at the very least, *wetiko* usually refers to people who cause terrible harm to others. I then went on to say that we can approach stories and accounts of the wetiko, as a legal concept or category, most effectively if we assume they describe reasoning people in reasoned legal orders, look for possible current uses of the principles, and recognize the universal or common human problem they represent. I am interested in finding if the legal principles in the *wetiko* stories and accounts can be usefully applied to the issues of internal violence and child victimization today.

In this chapter, I point out the similarities between the current thinking and theorizing about the dynamics of child victimization and the thinking and theorizing about the dynamics of the *wetiko* concept. Looking at both together shows there are strong similarities in how we understand the dynamics, including tactics, characteristics, and possible causes of both *wetiko*s and offenders in child victimization. The similarities between these dynamics are the basis for the next chapter, where I discuss the legal principles in the *wetiko* stories and accounts. These legal principles might help us think about how to protect our children from terrible harms caused by people close to us, and think about how to recognize and respond to people close to us who may cause terrible harm to others.

There are two important caveats (or cautions) about the content of this chapter. First, pointing out some of the thinking and theorizing about the dynamics of child victimization is not the same as being an expert on these dynamics. This chapter should not be read as a stand-alone guide to understanding or solving the difficult and complicated issue of child victimization. Second, pointing out the similarities between the dynamics of child victimization and the *wetiko* concept is not the same as arguing that addressing child victimization is then the *only* reasonable use for the *wetiko* principles. Several writers have used the *wetiko* concept to describe other pressing issues of our time, such as colonialism, imperialism, corporate greed, organized violence, terrorism, and war.[1] As pointed out in the last chapter, a complex concept like the *wetiko* can be used in many different, overlapping ways in different contexts, so it would be silly to reduce it to just one thing or another. I am not trying to do so here. With these cautions in mind, we now turn to the similarities between the thinking and theorizing about the dynamics of child victimization and the *wetiko*, including tactics, characteristics, and possible causes.

Tactics

*Wetiko*s have many tactics to get what they want and avoid being stopped. The *wetiko* stories remind us that victims are not to blame for being overpowered, tricked, or lured by someone intent on victimizing someone.

Brute Strength and Intimidation

The Wetiko: *Wetiko*s were terribly strong, and it took very strong people to stop them. Sometimes *wetiko*s used their powers to intimidate or force people into a vulnerable position. It is often said that the sound of a *wetiko*'s cry or yell could make people faint away.[2] Several stories

---

1 See Basil Johnston, *The Manitous: The Supernatural World of the Ojibway* (Toronto: Key Porter Books, 1995), 85; Jack D. Forbes, *Columbus and Other Cannibals: The Wetiko Disease of Exploitation, Imperialism and Terrorism*, rev. ed. (Toronto: Seven Stories, 2008), 42; and a recent war novel about two James Bay Cree men: Joseph Boyden, *Three Day Road* (Toronto: Penguin Books, 2005).

2 See Morton Teicher, "Windigo Psychosis: A Study of a Relationship between Belief and Behavior among the Indians of Northeastern Canada," in *Proceedings of the 1960 Annual Spring Meeting of the American Ethnological Society*, ed. Verne F. Ray (Seattle: University of Washington Press, 1960), 27 (Anishinabek) and 34; Interview 1: Interview of two anonymous elders, 11 April 2009, Alberta; and Interview 4, Interview of anonymous community leader, 13 June 2009, Alberta (Cree). See also Johnston, *Manitous*, 226, where a man who does not yet realize he has turned into a windigo giant calls out a welcome when he sees a village and most people drop dead. "The giant

recount the people needing to seek out, or the *wetiko* being bested by, people with strong medicine.[3] *Wetiko*s could uproot trees, and the strong men fought the *wetiko*s with whole trees.[4] In some stories, the *wetiko* tries to starve out the people. In one, the *wetiko* makes all the animals, and even some humans, appear as skeletons to the hunters.[5] In another, the *wetiko* steals all the fish and empties all the kettles of food.[6] In yet another, the *wetiko* shrinks all the animals into dwarf animals so small they come out of a man's mouth as he dreams.[7] In these stories, *wetiko*s use their strength and power to intimidate, paralyse, or weaken people through starvation. They do so in order to take advantage of their vulnerability to get what they want.

Child Victimization: In some cases of child victimization, an offender may use brute strength and terror.[8] There is no shame attached to being less strong than a *wetiko* or even paralysed in terror when he yells. There is no shame in a child being less strong than an adult, or being too paralysed with fear to resist. In the *wetiko* stories, the only solution is for a stronger person to help. The stronger person is able to resist the *wetiko* and protect the weaker ones. Similarly, children need strong adults

---

had meant no harm. All he meant to do was to let them know that he was in their land and was there on friendly business. But he had killed many of them, though he did not know it yet." When he sees the corpses, his hunger overtakes him and he eats them. It is at this point he becomes a *wetiko*, rather than just a giant.

3 See Teicher, "Windigo Psychosis," 37 and 39.

4 Ibid., 18–19.

5 Howard Norman, *Where the Chill Came From: Cree Windigo Tales and Journeys* (San Francisco: North Point, 1982), 69.

6 Ibid., 71.

7 Ibid., 110.

8 Offenders may use "overt coercion" to overcome a child's resistance. Rex Wild and Patricia Anderson, *Ampe Akelyernemane Meke Mekarle, "Little Children Are Sacred": Report of the Northern Territory Board of Inquiry into the Protection of Aboriginal Children from Sexual Abuse* (Darwin, AU: Northern Territory Government, 2007), s. 5. See also David Finkelhor, *Childhood Victimization: Violence, Crime and Abuse in the Lives of Young People* (New York: Oxford University Press, 2008), 75–7. Finkelhor explains the sexual victimization of a child is frequently a *"pain-mediated"* victimization, as distinguished from "purely meaning-mediated victimizations, such as theft" that "have no element of physical pain." While a negative meaning can occur simultaneously or develop over time, unmediated pain "for example – the forced penetration of a penis into an anus or vagina" and "other readily appraised noxious activities, such as threatening or restraining the child" are often components of the sexual victimization brought to the attention of authorities.

to protect them from other adults.[9] Children are rarely, if ever, strong enough to protect themselves on their own.

Creating Confusion, Distraction, or Fear

The *Wetiko*: *Wetiko*s don't just use brute strength and intimidation. They also use their power to weaken or distract people through confusion and fear. In one story, the *wetiko* creates a mud hole that takes a man's memory away in order to capture him.[10] Once, when hunters are looking for a fox, the *wetiko* makes foxes appear all around the horizons so it was confusing and difficult to know which one to follow.[11] Another *wetiko* uses a "many-voiced" moth to confuse and distract the man who has found his camp. The moth taunts the man that he will starve and echoes back the man's own voice, which makes him feel very alone and frightened.[12] In one story, the *wetiko* causes a famine, but makes everyone believe it is an owl's fault.[13] In another, the *wetiko* creates fear and worry by warning people it is dangerous to follow animal tracks – first hare, then moose – *after* someone is swallowed by the tracks.[14] Once, a *wetiko* tricks men looking for the *wetiko* to kill him, by mimicking the voice of a screech owl until they get used to it and sleep through it. In the morning they discover the *wetiko* had come right up to the camp and killed the man on watch.[15]

In the oral descriptive accounts, one elder, who practises traditional medicine, made the important point that it is not always the person becoming a *wetiko* who tries to confuse and distract others from guessing what is going on. Sometimes it is the person's family members. In one case, a man who did not speak Cree was brought to this elder and her husband for help. When they asked the man questions, it was clear to them he was talking, but the woman with him was not translating his answers. The elders told him they would help him, but only when

---

9 For example, some studies show incest offenders are less likely than other offenders to reoffend once their daughters are "older or well protected." See Finkelhor and Associates, *Sourcebook on Child Sexual Abuse*, 135.
10 Howard Norman, *Where the Chill Came From: Cree Windigo Tales and Journeys* (San Francisco: North Point, 1982), 34–5.
11 Ibid., 45.
12 Ibid., 48–9.
13 Ibid., 54.
14 Ibid., 62.
15 Ibid., 79–80.

they had their own translator. Once they made new arrangements, he answered all their questions, and they were able to determine what was happening to him. In another case, they were asked to help a woman several times over a period of years, first by her mother, then by her husband. While the elders suspected the woman was becoming a *wetiko*, her mother and husband dodged their questions and tried to keep things covered up. It was only after the woman and her husband moved away from her mother that the husband was honest about his wife's behaviours, perhaps because he was overwhelmed taking care of her on his own.

Child Victimization: In cases of child victimization, offenders seldom want others to know what they are doing, or to stop them from doing it. If someone confronts them or the child tells others, they may dismiss the capability and memory of the child, like the story of the mud hole.[16] They may lie about what is happening, or change the focus to distract people from what they are actually doing, like the *wetiko*s do with the foxes and the moths. They may try to avoid responsibility for their actions, like the *wetiko* blamed the owl for the famine.[17] Sometimes offenders try to make people feel isolated and afraid, like the moths do to the man. Or they try to make people too afraid of other people to realize the offender is the one to fear, like the *wetiko* who warns of the tracks after they swallow people up. Sometimes offenders "normalize" abusive behaviours towards women and children within a family or community, so that people might "sleep through" the signs, in the same way the *wetiko* normalized his cry until the men slept through it and he could kill one without the rest noticing.[18]

---

16 For example, claims that disclosures of sexual abuse are really "false accusations" or "false memories." See Katherine Beckett, "Culture and the Politics of Signification: The Case of Child Sexual Abuse," *Social Problems* 43, no. 1 (1996): 64.

17 Garry P. Perry and Janet Orchard, *Assessment and Treatment of Adolescent Sex Offenders* (Sarasota, FL: Professional Resource, 1992), 12. Offenders "use a variety of defense mechanisms (e.g., denial, rationalization, projection) to cope with their commission of aggressive or deviant acts." This includes beliefs such as "she must have wanted it because she didn't fight back" or the "victim seduced me," which allow the offender to blame the victim to avoid responsibility. To add an additional layer, they caution that families who may be physically or sexually abusing an adolescent offender may avoid "taking responsibility by blaming the offender" (13).

18 Finkelhor and Associates, *Sourcebook on Child Sexual Abuse*, 55; Wild and Anderson, *Ampe Akelyernemane Meke Mekarle*, s. 5.2; and John H. Hylton, *Aboriginal Sexual Offending in Canada*, 2nd ed. (Ottawa: Ontario Aboriginal Healing Foundation, 2006), 51–2. http://www.ahf.ca/downloads/revisedsexualoffending_reprint.pdf.

Just as the elder pointed out about her experience with the family members of people becoming a *wetiko*, it is not just the offender who might confuse and distract others to keep things hidden. Sometimes family members also do so. Family members might feel embarrassed or ashamed. It may feel unbearable to face the facts about someone they love. Some people talk about families even "organizing themselves" around chaos and crisis to avoid the pain of facing the abuse that is happening.[19] Some people believe this is happening at community levels, where social issues, such as high suicide rates and crippling substance abuse, are actually linked directly to the "perpetual denial of hidden pain, and perpetual fear of it ever being disclosed."[20] The Cree elder's experience shows that even when families or communities ask for help, they may not tell the whole story. Unfortunately, this means that even when there are people willing and able to help, they might not be able to do so effectively. Breaking the secrecy and silence is hard, but important.[21]

Luring Victims Close

The *Wetiko*: Sometimes the *wetiko* tricks people into coming to him so he can eat them. In one story, strange moss grows, and during the night one man hears the wind calling his name. When he goes to climb a mysteriously moss-covered waterfall, the wind swirls the moss over him, trapping him underneath. When the other men wake up, they "saw it was a Windigo trying to trap Nepaskaw under the moss, to save him to eat later."[22] Another time, a man grows ill and hears rain, even though

---

19 Richard Kagan and Shirley Schlosberg, *Families in Perpetual Crisis* (Markham, ON: Penguin Books, 1989), 8–9. Kagan and Schlosberg use the image of "a family dancing rapidly around a pit of emptiness – a black hole. This pit holds the ghosts and horrors of hidden traumas (past and present) which the family cannot face or resolve" (9). This can lead to chaotic and frightening environments, where family members "appear mired in repetitive cycles of denial and of aggressive or self-destructive behaviors which perpetuate conflicts, crises, and vulnerabilities to trauma" (15).

20 Rupert Ross, "Traumatization in Remote First Nations: An Expression of Concern" (2006), 4 (author's collection). Ross gives the example of a chief and council suddenly withdrawing funding to send sixteen young men to a treatment centre rather than jail when they learned the focus would be on the sexual abuse they had all suffered as children.

21 However, Hylton stresses, "If victims are encouraged to disclose the abuse they have suffered, adequate and appropriate services must be available for victims and offenders. If not, many will be left even more severely damaged." See Hylton, *Aboriginal Sexual Offending in Canada*, 140.

22 Norman, *Where the Chill Came From*, 84.

it is not raining. The *wetiko*, disguised as an old man, comes to see him and talks about rain. Later, when the man hears the rain again, he asks his companions, "Get the old man. We have to speak about rain." The old man appeared without being called, and the ill man leaves with him on his own volition. The *wetiko* kills him.[23] In one story, a hermit arrives at a village and says he needs an apprentice to come away with him, so he can teach them all he knows before he dies. No one remembered him except for one old man, Wawao. When the hermit appeared, Wawao said, "It's you!" They looked at each other a long time with anger. The hermit asked someone to come with him again, but "seeing Wawao's anger, no one would go with the hermit." Later, Wawao kills the hermit and tells everyone he was a *wetiko*.[24]

One of the most interesting stories about this *wetiko* tactic is the one in which a fox speaks to a man named Nuneskapew, who heard about the fox from an elder, Niskepeme, who had known and spoke fondly of the fox from his childhood. The fox begins to appear around Nuneskapew's village, each day speaking to one elder or another and each day speaking to Nuneskapew. It turns out the fox does not "belong to anyone's childhood" yet. Nuneskapew wants the fox to tell him things for his memory, but the fox keeps stalling. The elders ask if the fox has warned Nuneskapew that he is working for a *wetiko*, but Nuneskapew "wanted the fox for his memory too badly to believe it." Nuneskapew sets out alone to talk to the fox at night, but all through the night, every time he falls asleep, he wakes up to find one elder, then another elder sleeping there. In the morning when everyone wakes up, they hear the *wetiko* coming. One elder tells him, "There is a reason that fox you spoke with was never taken for anyone's memory." Together they conjure to kill the *wetiko*. Once the *wetiko* is dead, they leave Nuneskapew alone. When the fox comes back and learns the *wetiko* is dead, the fox "began telling Nuneskapew a lot of useful things."[25]

Child Victimization: These *wetiko* tactics are particularly important to recognize, because in cases of child victimization, offenders often use tricks to bring children closer to them or make children trust them so they can victimize them. This is called "grooming." They may take advantage of children's natural curiosity or interest, like the *wetiko* did

---

23 Ibid., 119–20.
24 Ibid., 112–14. He conjures himself into a weasel and eats the windigo's heart.
25 Ibid., 36–9.

to the man who climbed the moss-covered waterfall. They may befriend a child, and convince the child that they understand like no one else can, like the *wetiko* did with the rain and the ill man.[26] The offender may orchestrate things so the child will choose to go with them alone, just like the *wetiko* did with the ill man.[27] An offender may offer to be helpful to a family and child, just like the old hermit who turned out to be a *wetiko*.[28] Many Indigenous people already know that outsiders offering to teach their children many useful things may turn out to be offenders, because of the residential schools.

The story of the childhood fox is different, because the fox is familiar. In the case of the old hermit, Wawao speaks angrily to him so everyone stays away from him. In the case of the childhood fox, Nuneskapew is first drawn to the fox because Niskepeme had talked about the fox fondly. People with whom we are familiar and fond of can be offenders. In fact, in 80–90 per cent of child victimizations, the offender is a family member or friend.[29] It is almost impossible to live in constant distrust of family and friends. Nevertheless, there will always be people, like the fox, willing to exploit this trust.[30] In this story of the childhood fox, the elders demonstrate powerful ways to prevent offences. They keep talking to both the fox and Nuneskapew. When the elders find out the fox has not told Nuneskapew he is working for the *wetiko*, and see that Nuneskapew

---

26 Gregory M. Weber, "Grooming Children for Sexual Abuse," TULIR, Centre for the Prevention & Healing of Child Sexual Abuse, http://www.tulir.org/grooming.htm.
  Offenders often "engage" or "recruit" their victims in different ways. Many use a combination of charm and "bonding." They may offer to play games, give rides, or buy treats and gifts as tokens of friendship. "They may offer drugs or alcohol to older children or teenagers. And they almost always offer a sympathetic, understanding ear."

27 Wild and Anderson, *Ampe Akelyernemane Meke Mekarle*, s. 6.4. "The vast majority of offenders will attempt to lure a child away from the scrutiny of others."

28 Ibid. Child sex offenders "gain access to children through a variety of means, creating opportunities to be alone with a child by forming friendships and intimate relationships with single parents and via their employment (e.g., child care worker, teacher), or by participating in volunteer activities involving children."

29 Finkelhor, *Childhood Victimization*, 47; and Carol-Ann Bauman, "The Sentencing of Sexual Offences against Children," *Criminal Reports* 17 (1998): 360. In a study of 1,113 sexual abuse sentencing cases, Bauman found that 96 per cent involved a position of trust, 51 per cent involved a father or a father figure, and 21 per cent involved a relative.

30 Finkelhor, *Childhood Victimization*, 48. Finkelhor believes that, while education may help, we will likely never overcome the tendency to "underestimate the dangers posed by families and friends." This is because family life and friendship networks "cannot operate without trust and assumptions of reciprocity."

wants the fox for his memory too badly to listen to believe them, they make sure they protect him with their presence. After they kill the *wetiko*, they do leave Nuneskapew with the fox, and he does learn many useful things. Similarly, a child may not believe warnings when he or she wants to be with someone very badly. Safe adults need to stay present and provide protection when they recognize the danger the child may not see.[31] The child might still gain good things from these relationships with others present for protection or after the danger is removed.

Wetiko Characteristics

If *wetiko*s were still giants, it would be easy to recognize one. However, in the written and oral descriptive accounts, *wetiko*s are people, or the account is about a person who is turning into a *wetiko*. We need to identify these characteristics in order to recognize someone fitting into the broad category of a *wetiko*, or who is in a state where he or she might harm others in ways analogous to the "ideal type" *wetiko*. Some people might already recognize characteristics signalling that someone is not safe to be around today. However, I am not saying that this is automatically so. These are theories that help guide judgment, rather than a math equation.

Lack of Self-Care, Self-Destructiveness, and Sadness

The *Wetiko*: In the older stories, signs that someone was dangerous or at risk of becoming dangerous included self-destructiveness, a lack of self-care, and deep sadness or brooding. In some stories, a *wetiko* "literally ate its own lips."[32] One elder I interviewed thinks that this symptom is likely the result of a curse.[33] Some people described a complete lack of self-care.[34]

In addition, in several accounts, the person becoming a *wetiko* is described as suffering from "melancholia" or as consumed with "sad thoughts."[35]

---

31 Weber, "Grooming Children for Sexual Abuse." "The best way to recognize grooming behavior is to pay attention to your child and the people in your child's life. Children require the protection of adults, usually from adults. Their intuition is not yet developed with enough information and experience to keep them from harm."

32 Candice Savage, ed., *The World of Wetiko: Tales from the Woodland Cree, as Told by Marie Merasty* (Saskatoon, SK: Saskatchewan Indian Cultural College, 1974), 3.

33 Interview 1.

34 Savage, *World of Wetiko*, 3.

35 J.B. Tyrell, ed., *David Thompson's Narratives* (1916), 125–6, in Teicher, "Windigo Psychosis," 81.

Richard Preston explains the *wetiko* "is not necessarily a cannibal; he may be only a murderer of his fellows, urged on by dreams, melancholy, and brooding.[36] While in some stories, there seems to be some sympathy for such behaviour, one person I interviewed explained that brooding and self-isolation was a choice to give in or spend too much time with one's own dark side, rather than asking for help right away. This let dark things develop and then other people had to step in to "clean up the mess."[37]

Child Victimization: In the case of child victimization, we must take great care not to say everyone who is sad, self-destructive, or not caring for themselves is dangerous. Just as the Cree elder speculated about the eating of one's own lips being caused by a curse, sometimes self-destructiveness is the result of someone being victimized. Not everybody or even most people who have been victimized go on to victimize other people.[38] However, sometimes when people stop caring for themselves, do self-destructive things, and seem to be "drowning in self-pity," they may no longer care if they harm other people.[39] For example, there are some people I will visit when they are physically clean and sober, but whom I steer clear of when I see them with messy hair and dirty clothes, because I know they are on a drug or alcohol binge, and often no longer themselves. They may hurt me or someone else in that state, and not even remember it when they sober up.

Distorted and Obsessive Thoughts and Wants

The *Wetiko*: Other characteristics of someone becoming a *wetiko* are distorted thoughts and wants. Sometimes people lose their appetite for regular food. Someone turning into a *wetiko* might stop eating and refuse any food.[40] Some people believed that "once a person had eaten human flesh, he found other foods distasteful."[41] Some people

---

36 Norman, *Where the Chill Came From*, 3.
37 Interview 4.
38 Finkelhor and Associates, *Sourcebook on Child Sexual Abuse*, 121: "It is clear that being molested in itself is not enough to create a molester. Otherwise all those who were molested would ... become molesters. We know from clinical histories that this is not the case. In fact, it is probable that only a *small* percentage of victims go on to be abusers."
39 One cognitive distortion addressed in sexual offender treatment is offenders' maintenance of "low opinions of themselves." Perry and Orchard, *Assessment and Treatment*, 12.
40 Teicher, "Windigo Psychosis," 64.
41 Savage, *World of Wetiko*, 3.

hallucinated, seeing other humans as animals acceptable to eat, and repeatedly obsessed about or dreamed of eating people.

One man becoming a *wetiko* through a curse "could not hunt, eat or sleep. Fastening his eyes on his [pregnant] wife's stomach ... he claimed he saw a beaver in the uterus."[42] Another man eats his wife and children after he sees his wife "all covered with blood, running toward him."[43] In yet another case, the woman would only see her husband and children, because strangers "became metamorphosed in her eyes into wild animals – wolves, bears, lynxes. These animals are dangerous to life. To protect herself she was driven by the desire to kill them. But this was repugnant to her, because these 'animals' are human beings."[44] Other accounts speak of seeing people as fat ptarmigans or beavers.[45]

Sometimes the desire to eat human flesh is undisguised. Cannibalism was "often, but not always" one aspect of "going Windigo."[46] This was both a precursor to someone becoming *wetiko*,[47] and a continuing obsession that contributed to the repetition of the offence. For example, in one case, an old man even reportedly dug up a cemetery, looking for more human flesh.[48] If we accept the view that dreams were an "experiential phenomenon" and could "instigate action,"[49] then this category can be broadened to include the stories in which someone continually dreams he or she becomes a *wetiko*.

I am aware that some observers explain *wetiko* dreams as a cause of *wetiko* behaviour, rather than a characteristic.[50] However, this does not match the interpretation of that causal relationship in my interviews in northern Alberta. Dreams are not interpreted as a causal factor, but rather as a signal for the dreamer to tell someone and seek help before

---

42 Teicher, "Windigo Psychosis," 59.

43 Ibid., 76.

44 J.E. Saindon, "Mental Disorders among the James Bay Cree," *Primitive Man* 6 (1933): 1–12, in Teicher, "Windigo Psychosis," 89–90.

45 Norman, *Where the Chill Came From*, 4, citing Isaac Greys, a Cree elder.

46 Ibid., 3.

47 See Henry Y. Hind, *Explorations in the Interior of the Labrador Peninsula* (London: Longman, Green, Longman, Roberts and Green, 1863), in Teicher, "Windigo Psychosis," 103.

48 Teicher, "Windigo Psychosis," 84.

49 Ibid., 105.

50 Jennifer S.H. Brown and Robert Brightman, *The Orders of the Dreamed: George Nelson on Cree and Northern Ojibwa Religion and Myth, 1923* (Winnipeg: University of Manitoba Press, 1990), 90.

it is too late in the *wetiko* transformation.[51] In my interviews, I was told that the person who has such a dream (or other *wetiko* symptoms) has a responsibility to tell someone about it and seek help. There is help available if it is wanted.[52] Someone who does not seek or accept help after such a dream is choosing a dangerous course of action by delving into and indulging in the dark side.[53]

In one account, a woman reported being alarmed enough to kill her husband after she saw him drinking raw blood, because he "often told her he dreamt he would become a man-eater."[54] George Nelson saw *wetiko* dreams as one cause for becoming *wetiko*. However, he himself relates a story of a man who tells of a dream where a stranger tries to get him to eat food that he realizes is human meat, so refuses. The man says, "Had I unfortunately eaten of this, then had I become a cannibal in addition to all my other misfortunes."[55] The man exercises agency and makes a choice not to eat the meat in his dream. Nelson says that those who do eat at such a dream feast are "frequently, but not universally told thus: 'This is a sign to Thee that thou shalt one day become a cannibal and feed on the flesh of thy fellows – when thou shalt see children play with, and eat ice (or snow) *in* thy Tent, say, "my time is near"; for then thou shalt soon eat *indian* (human) flesh.'" He also reports they often immediately seek out a medicine person upon having such a dream.[56] While the language of "shalt" sounds like a cause, the frequent immediate next step, when set beside the preventive execution by the wife in the first account, reinforces the interpretation of what dreams mean in relation to turning into a *wetiko* in the interviews. Those who seek help do not become a *wetiko*. However, if they continue to indulge in dreaming the dreams without seeking help, they may.

Child Victimization: In the case of child victimization, an offender's thoughts and obsessions matter more than we might imagine. In particular, sexual offender treatment and relapse prevention focuses on recognizing and changing patterns of "distorted" sexual desires, fantasies,

---

51 Interview 1.
52 Ibid.; and Interview 4.
53 Interview 4.
54 M. Duncan Cameron, "The Nipigan Country, 1804," in *Les Bourgeois de la Campagnie du Nord-Ouest*, ed. L.R. Masson (Quebec: A. Coté, 1890), 249–50, in Teicher, "Windigo Psychosis," 104.
55 Brown and Brightman, *Orders of the Dreamed*, 90.
56 Ibid., 91.

and obsessions.[57] This often involves intense group work, journaling, and education about healthy sexuality and consensual sexual interactions.[58] Like the people who saw humans, who should not be eaten, as animals, such as beavers or ptarmigans, who can be eaten, some theorists believe sexual offenders see children, who should not be sexualized or sexually related to, as "appropriate objects of sexual interest"[59] or capable of being consensual sexual partners.[60]

Most sexual offenders obsess about and plan their offences for a long time before they actually act.[61] Like the people who obsess or dream about eating humans, if they do not seek help, they might go too far and cause great harm to real people. Like the people who seek help immediately after having a *wetiko* dream, offenders who recognize their pattern and seek help when they start obsessing about inappropriate sexual acts or partners can, with planning and knowledgeable support, stop the thinking pattern before they hurt anyone.[62]

Process and Progression over Time

The *Wetiko*: Finally, no one ever wakes up one day as a *wetiko*. Becoming a *wetiko* clearly always takes some time, from days, to a season, to years, in some cases. In one account, a Cree elder described a young man who was brought to him for help as saying he was "wandering

---

57 See Hylton, *Aboriginal Sexual Offending*, 102. The "most commonly used and widely evaluated" treatment approach to sexual offenders is cognitive-behavioural therapies. This therapy focuses on three goals: "[1] Changing the person's maladaptive pattern of deviant arousal, [2] correcting the distorted thought patterns that support these maladaptive behaviours, and [3] increasing the person's social competence."
58 Ibid., 103. See also Perry and Orchard, *Assessment and Treatment*, 67–92, for a more detailed description of group therapy components.
59 Finkelhor and Associates, *Sourcebook on Childhood Sexual Abuse*, 95.
60 A vital part of cognitive behavioural approaches to offender treatment is "addressing cognitive distortions," which include "false and distorted beliefs that offenders rely on to justify or minimize their behaviours." See Hylton, *Aboriginal Sexual Offending*, 102.
61 Perry and Orchard, *Assessment and Treatment*, 8.
62 This is the importance of a relapse prevention programs. Hylton, *Aboriginal Sexual Offending*, 104. In these programs, an offender learns "the patterns of thinking, feeling and behaving that have contributed to their offending in the past. The sex offender then makes a plan to avoid the triggers that increases his risk of reoffending … strategies for controlling behavior are learned and rehearsed."

toward killing someone."[63] Norman explains that the "Windigo-spirit inside that person evolves and amplifies in ferocity." Once someone begins to change, it "gets worse and worse."[64] While the transformation could be sudden, it generally progressed over at least a season.[65] In some cases, the progression into a *wetiko* took years.[66] There was time to ask for help. One elder explained that if she could sense this was beginning to happen to someone, she would approach him privately first, and ask if he needed or wanted help. If he did, she would help. If not, she would have to tell people for safety reasons.[67]

Child Victimization: Similarly, no one wakes up one day and is suddenly an offender, a drug dealer, or a murderer. There is always a process to get to that point. This can be a progression, just like the *wetiko* spirit might evolve and amplify inside a person becoming a *wetiko*. Most sexual offenders have offending patterns that escalate in "frequency and severity" over time, if not stopped.[68] However, it is worth asking whether the help and support is always there to stop the escalation. The elder in the interview approached the person she sensed was at risk and asked if he needed or wanted help. If he did, she helped him. In contrast, for some children, lots of people will gossip about them or their parents, but no one steps forward to ask if they need help. In many communities, the resources for help are simply not available, even if people sincerely want it.[69]

---

63 Norman, *Where the Chill Came From*, 11, quoting Cree elder Jason Crow.

64 Ibid., 5, citing Cree elder Samuel Makidemewabe.

65 Interview 4.

66 See, for example, the case of the woman who hid this condition for years, in Interview 1; and the case of Wiskahoo, who would start talking about turning into a *wetiko* only when he was drunk, and was simply tied up in these times for a period of three years before he became too dangerous, in Tyrell, *David Thompson's Narrative*, 126.

67 Interview 1.

68 Perry and Orchard, *Assessment and Treatment*, 1. Some studies have shown the "severity of offending behaviour may escalate when there is no treatment." In a study of incarcerated adult offenders, "35% reported progression from compulsive masturbation, exhibitionism, and voyeurism as youths to the more serious sexually aggressive behaviors for which they had been convicted as adults" (4).

69 McGillivray and Comaskey report "a near-fatal lack of resources" facing women and children in situations of intimate violence in reserve communities. Anne McGillivray and Brenda Comaskey, *Black Eyes All of the Time: Intimate Violence, Aboriginal Women, and the Justice System* (Toronto: University of Toronto Press, 1999), 79.

Possible Causes for Turning into a *Wetiko*

When something terrible or terrifying happens, it is normal for people affected to want to know why it happened. This is part of our human reaction to trauma. We want a simple explanation we can understand because the trauma has shattered our trust in our world and the people in it.[70] Unfortunately, there are usually no simple answers to a "why" question when it comes to violence and victimization. The *wetiko* is no exception. As one community leader pointed out to me, the reasons behind someone becoming a *wetiko* are never "purely this or purely that."[71] Similarly, experts on offenders say that there is no simple answer to the question of why a particular person becomes an offender. It is always a multi-factored process that defies simple explanations.[72]

Still, several people suggest possible causes for becoming a *wetiko*. These are important to review because they may suggest preventive strategies, and help us understand the dynamics at play in some cases. However, none of them should be viewed as standalone causal factors. These are ongoing puzzles of our human condition.

Starvation and Suffering

The *Wetiko*: Some people believed that people became a *wetiko* if they were forced to eat human flesh if they were starving. Norman explains people became *wetiko* "often in a time of great stress due to acute hunger."[73] One elder explains her belief that if a hunter could not find game, he might "kill and eat what he could … [but f]rom the moment he began to eat human flesh, he was a true *Wetiko*."[74] David Thompson speculates in his journals about the reasoning behind this assumption in a Cree context: "As the strong affection of an Indian is centered in his children, for they may be said to be all he has to depend upon, they believe the dreadful distressed state of mind which necessity forces on them to take the life of one of their children to preserve the others leaves such a sad

---

70 Judith Herman, *Trauma and Recovery: The Aftermath of Violence; From Domestic Violence to Political Terror* (New York: Basic Books, 1997), 51; and Finkelhor, *Childhood Victimization*, 23.

71 Interview 4.

72 Finkelhor and Associates, *Sourcebook on Child Sexual Abuse*, 121.

73 Norman, *Where the Chill Came From*, 3.

74 Savage, *World of Wetiko*, 1.

indelible impression that the parents are never again the same as they were before, and are liable to aberrations of mind."[75]

George Nelson speculates in his journals, a little less sympathetically, that "those who have once preyed upon their fellows, ever after feel a great desire for the same nourishment, and are not so scrupulous about the means of procuring it."[76] One elder I interviewed speculated there are fewer *wetikos* today because there is less starvation and it is warmer.[77]

As the journals of David Thompson suggest, closely related and overlapping with this cause is that the belief that *wetiko* behaviours are the result of great physical or mental suffering. One account explains a man's murder of his wife as "the result of a state of delirium, produced by his suffering."[78] One voyageur assessed that his friend, Missabikongs, was not yet a *wetiko*, but might become one if he were "driven mad by his sufferings."[79] In the case of Marie Courtereille, one explanation of her starting to become a *wetiko* is that the loss of six out of nine of her children, within a five-year period, "affected her mind."[80]

Child Victimization: Today, when looking at child victimization, we must acknowledge that while there is little actual starvation anymore, there is widespread and entrenched poverty in Indigenous communities.[81] There are no fast answers to this now, but if suffering and deprivation does contribute to victimization, then this logically suggests improving life conditions and reducing social suffering may lessen the incidence of violence and victimization in future generations.[82]

---

75 Tyrell, *David Thompson's Narrative*, 125–6.

76 Brown and Brightman, *Orders of the Dreamed*, 88.

77 Interview 4, 32.

78 J.D. Kohl, *Kitchi-Gami, Wanderings round Lake Superior* (London: Chapman and Hall, 1860), in Teicher, "Windigo Psychosis," 50.

79 Ibid., 51.

80 Nathan Carlson, "Appendix Cases," in "Reviving the Wihtikow: Cannibal Monsters in Northern Alberta Cree and Metis Cosmology" (BA thesis, University of Alberta, 2005) (author's collection), 107. Carlson reports, "Six of her children died before 1885; 4 of which tragically passed away in 1884." Courtereille was killed in 1887.

81 Turpel-Lafond argues that "lateral violence" in Indigenous communities is "clearly impacted by poverty and dislocation." See Mary Ellen Turpel-Lafond, "Some Thoughts on Inclusion and Innovation in the Saskatchewan Justice System," *Saskatchewan Law Review* 68 (2005): 295.

82 Wild and Anderson, *Ampe Akelyernemane Meke Mekarle*, s. 6.3. But see Finkelhor, *Childhood Victimization*, 50, who suggests there is a more complicated relationship between poverty and abuse than usually thought. He cites a 2003 study that found that risk was not increased by "racial composition, poverty, or central city location."

At this point, there may be very few Indigenous people in Canada who have not endured or witnessed immense suffering in their lives. In the residential schools, some children may have been forced, or seen no other choice, to act in horrible ways to others in order to survive. This can happen within families too. Some people may have internalized this terrible shame, and given up hope, as David Thompson suggests,[83] or they may have developed a taste for the momentary power and satisfaction these actions provide, like George Nelson suggests.[84] Many people believe that children who have been victimized are more likely to victimize others when they are adults.[85] However, current evidence shows most people who are victimized do *not* go on to victimize others.[86] As well, some offenders have not been offended against.[87] Care must be taken not to add to victims' burden of stigma and fear by accepting a "single-cause" intergenerational theory of offending.[88] Suffering may contribute, but does not cause offending on its own.

Abuse, Misuse, or Loss of Power

The *Wetiko*: In some stories, people begin to turn *wetiko* because of others' purposefully bad use of or even accidental lack of care for their medicine power. Turning *wetiko* can also be seen as related to a person giving up personal power, giving in to selfishness or the dark side. Issues of power are complex and always debatable, but there is no doubt we all have the power to affect our own and others' lives.

---

83 Rupert Ross, *Returning to the Teachings: Exploring Aboriginal Justice* (Toronto: Penguin Books, 1996), 43, gives his view that abuse can have a generational aspect, that some victims may "try to compensate for their own degradation by degrading others."

84 Wild and Anderson, *Ampe Akelyernemane Meke Mekarle*, s. 4.3, point out studies that show sex offenders are more likely to view their own abuse as "normal," and sometimes enjoyable, than the non-offending sample of abuse victims. This may suggest "the normalization of sexual abuse via denial or repression of traumatic aspects and acceptance of pleasurable aspects may enable … offenders … to rationalize away the damage they do when sexually abusing children."

85 Ibid. This is especially prevalent in popular explanations of sexual offending.

86 Ibid.; and Finkelhor and Associates, *Sourcebook on Child Sexual Abuse*, 121.

87 Finkelhor and Associates, *Sourcebook on Child Sexual Abuse*, 121.

88 Ibid., 123: "The idea that victims grow up to be abusers has struck terror into the hearts of victims, in particular male victims, and their parents. These people, now even more than in the past, have the unrealistic and unnecessary fear that they or their children are destined to become abusers. Although not a possibility to be ignored

In one story, an old Cree man gets mad when he hears a woman laugh because he thinks she is making fun of him. He curses her, and although she does not hear him, she becomes "sick and crazy" before Christmas. In this story, her mother cures her and the old man dies within four days, to everyone's great relief.[89] In another, a man marries a shaman's daughter against his wishes and the shaman chases him with a knife and "threaten[s] to send starvation on him."[90] Soon, "the evil came to pass ... and the son took to his bed." His wife cures him with "tender nursing."[91] In another, a "dread shaman," who "won his miserably fearful wife ... through love medicine" is mean and jealous, once even stabbing her in the chest. He accuses her of cheating with another man, although she hadn't. The other man gets mad and uses "bad spirits and bad medicine" to make the shaman into a *wetiko*. Here, white men take him, tie him up, and give him a drink of alcohol, but eventually he is taken to his son's home and his wife comes there too. He "was like that for four years. He died crazy."[92]

In another case, an evil sorcerer turns a young girl into a *wetiko* so he can have her as his wife once she eats her family. She has no memory of this, but one of the older wives pushes her to ask the sorcerer what happened. When he finally tells her, she becomes very depressed, chilled, and hungry for human flesh. Finally she hurls herself into a fire she has built herself.[93] However, bad intent with medicine power is not necessary. In one interview in northern Alberta, it was explained to me that the process of turning into a *wetiko* could be started by exposure to medicines that were stored or used carelessly. Even if someone starts the *wetiko* process because she snooped around and took a medicine she shouldn't have, part of the responsibility for her actions lies with the person who improperly stored the medicines. If the medicine was that powerful, it should have been hidden better against foreseeable risks like this.[94]

---

completely, these fears are almost certainly exaggerated." Not knowing the other contingencies involved prevents targeting concerns or providing useful guidance. "It is even possible that the fear itself has some self-fulfilling properties that may prompt some children to become molesters who would not otherwise have done so."

89 Ruth Landes, *The Ojibwa Woman* (New York: Columbia University Press, 1938), 194–5, in Teicher, "Windigo Psychosis," 58.

90 Ibid., 59.

91 Ibid.

92 Teicher, "Windigo Psychosis," 60.

93 Johnston, *Manitous*, 227–30. This is a rare case (Johnston says the only one) where "a weendigo killed itself to turn on its creator" (230).

94 Interview 4.

Child Victimization: In the case of child victimization, Indigenous people are struggling under the "curse" of both deliberate and blind misuses of power. Again, the residential school legacy is a good example. In the stories of people using bad medicine, the person misusing his power often ends up beaten or thwarted in his bad intentions. This is usually accomplished through the loving care of the relatives of the affected person, and their willingness to fight for her. Little Warriors, a charitable organization founded to prevent and respond to child sexual victimization, states that a similar "relentless compassion" by loved ones is needed today if children are to be safe and healthy.[95] At the same time, as pointed out in the interview about responsibility for the careless storage of medicines, the government's responsibility for the current situation should not be ignored.

The *Wetiko*: Another take on the relationship between people's power and turning *wetiko* can be found in Robin Ridington's comparative analysis of the Dunne-za concept of a *wechugo*, which occurs when someone becomes too powerful, and the *wetiko* concept, which he argues occurs when someone gives up power.[96] Johnston theorizes that the root of turning *wetiko* is giving in to the weakness of "selfishness, regarded by the Anishinaubae people as the worst human shortcoming."[97] The usual way a human being could become a *wetiko* is "by his or her own excesses."[98] Johnston describes a *wetiko* as someone who is endowed with "an abnormal craving, creating an internal imbalance to such a degree as to create a physical disorder. The Weendigo has no other object in life but to satisfy this lust and hunger, expending all its energy on this one purpose. As long as its lust and hunger are satisfied, nothing else matters – not compassion, sorrow, reason, or judgement."[99] In a similar line, one interviewee for this project stressed his opinion that people became *wetiko*s by choice, by choosing to delve too deeply and for too long into the dark side.[100]

---

95 The charitable organization focuses on educating adults to "help prevent, recognize and react responsibly" to child sexual abuse. Little Warriors, http://www.littlewarriors.ca/.

96 See generally, Robin Ridington, "Wechuge and Windigo: A Comparison of Cannibal Belief among Boreal Forest Athapaskans and Algonquians," in *Little Bit Know Something: Stories in the Language of Anthropology* (Vancouver: Douglas and McIntyre, 1990), 160–81.

97 Johnston, *Manitous*, 223.

98 Ibid., 227.

99 Ibid., 224.

100 Interview 4.

Child Victimization: These theories about power and the *wetiko* overlap with current theories and debates about the dynamics of child victimization. Some people see child victimization as resulting from an imbalance of power within families or societies. Family dynamics theorists argue that children are often victimized when one adult in the family has too much power, like the *wechugo*,[101] and another feels powerless or gives up the power, like the *wetiko,* or when there is general chaos and no one uses the power consistently or appropriately.[102] Feminist theorists argue child victimization is a result of an imbalance of power in the larger society, with too much within the hands of men, rather than just within families.[103] No one really knows for sure.

People struggle to understand child sexual victimization. A recent study of judges' descriptions of offenders' actions in sentencing showed that many judges see the cause of this victimization as being similar to the "usual cause" of *wetiko* behaviour described by Johnston – that is, an offender acting to satisfy his or her selfish desires with no thought or compassion for others.[104] This may be a choice to give in to one's dark side, as argued in the interview, or it could be an internal imbalance, a mental illness, or a personality disorder. In addition, we know an absence of "compassion, sorrow, reason, or judgement" can be the result of brain damage, from fetal alcohol spectrum disorder, or substance or solvent abuse. A combination of this absence, for any reason, combined with the "curse" of being victimized can create very dangerous people.[105] Again, it is important to remember these are all just theories. Issues of power and choice are complex in both the *wetiko* stories and in child victimization.

---

101 Wild and Anderson, *Ampe Akelyernemane Meke Mekarle,* s. 5.2, discussing the possibility "child sexual abuse may, like child physical abuse, occur as a function of the misuse of personal power."

102 Ibid., ss 4.3, 5.

103 Ibid., s. 5; Finkelhor and Associates, *Sourcebook on Child Sexual Abuse,* 113.

104 Clare MacMartin and Linda A. Wood, "Sexual Motives and Sentencing: Judicial Discourse in Cases of Child Sexual Abuse," *Journal of Language and Social Psychology* 24, no. 2 (2005): 145. "Explanations sometimes referred to how the crimes demeaned and degraded victims whose own needs and interests were sacrificed in order to satisfy the offenders' sexual desires."

105 See Ross, "Traumatization in Remote First Nations," 4.

Prolonged Isolation or Group Contagion

The *Wetiko*: Finally, *wetiko* behaviour has been linked, conversely, to prolonged isolation or to group contagion. On the one hand, extended isolation, whether forced or chosen, can contribute to becoming a *wetiko*. Norman explains that *wetiko*s are sometimes referred to as "He-who-lives-alone," or Upayokwitigo, roughly "hermit witigo." He relates three stories about hermits turning out to be *wetiko*s.[106] He says that bad shamans would occasionally isolate a person, and that such forced, prolonged isolation is said to make a person "go Windigo."[107] In the interviews, one sign that someone was giving in to the dark side was the choice to isolate himself or herself rather than ask for or accept help.[108]

On the other hand, there are accounts of many people, even whole communities, engaged in cannibalism during times of starvation. Teicher argues that in some cases, "the aberrant behaviour was made temporarily acceptable by the fact a number of people participated in it"[109] and that, when more than one individual participated, the deviant behaviour "became a temporary norm and for the immediate situation was shared, acceptable behaviour."[110] He likens group contagion to "accounts of mob violence."[111] In one case, where a *wetiko* grandmother and aunt constantly try to force their grandson/nephew to eat human meat, Teicher suggests some people might demonstrate a "purposeful effort to have others share in their cannibalistic desires," because "the intolerable act becomes more bearable if it is more widely shared. The greater the extent of participation, the more widespread is the burden of responsibility."[112]

---

106 Norman, *Where the Chill Comes From*, 121–2. See "The Hermit's Apprentice Windigo," 112–14; "The Tent Owl Windigo," 118–20; and "The Caribou-Hermit Windigo," 121–2.

107 Ibid., 4.

108 Interviews 1 and 4.

109 Teicher, "Windigo Psychosis," 48, referring to Brule Lake, otherwise known as "Win-de-go" Lake, where, in 1811 a band of around forty Ojibways, starving, apparently lived off the dead, until only one woman remained. She was executed upon meeting a larger group.

110 He "was a British officer who came to Canada in 1870 to join the Red River expedition." W.F. Butler (1874), 175–6n, in Teicher, "Windigo Psychosis," 53, referring to a man in a canoe described to him as a Windigo, for once eating up to forty others with others in his starving band.

111 Ibid., 57.

112 Ibid., 55.

Child Victimization: Today, in the case of child victimization, adults may face the tragic decision between risking placing a child in forced isolation or subjecting him or her to group contagion. Just as when *wetiko*-like behaviour became temporarily acceptable when more than one person did it, violence and victimization can seem like the norm when a child sees most people as either violent or victimized.[113] Even worse, just like the *wetiko* grandma and aunt who try to force their grandson/nephew to eat human meat, some offenders force others to watch or participate in acts of sexual and other victimization.[114] This happened in the residential schools. It can also happen in families and even in communities. Children should not be subjected to this.

At the same time, there is a long history of loss and loneliness that has resulted from Indigenous children being placed away from family and community. Their isolation and feelings of never belonging can feed into despair and a lack of attachment. Some children who act out their confusion and rage end up being shuffled from home to home, with no safe place at all. Some people might say these children have "attachment disorder."[115] These children often seem to feel nothing, think nothing of other people. Still, staying in the community is no guarantee against isolation. Some children are forced to fend for themselves at a very young age. They may end up being victimized by multiple offenders, and begin to act out.[116] This can also lead to attachment disorders, and being shunned or rejected by everyone around them. In the case of

---

113 Wild and Anderson, *Ampe Akelyernemane Meke Mekarle*, s. 6.3, citing a study that argues this generation of children have "been socialised into a culture of alcohol, substance abuse, violence and anarchy." See also Ross, "Traumatization in Remote First Nations."

114 See, for example, the case study of "Carl" presented by Ross, "Traumatization in Remote First Nations," 43.

115 Jeffrey J. Haugaard and Cindy Hazan, "Recognizing and Treating Uncommon Behavioral and Emotional Disorders in Children and Adolescents Who Have Been Severely Maltreated: Reactive Attachment Disorder," *Child Maltreatment* 9 (2004): 154.

116 The latest research on child victimization suggests that children who have experienced multiple victimizations demonstrate the most distress, have the worst adult outcomes, and are the most vulnerable to being victimized in the future. See Finkelhor, *Childhood Victimization*, 35 and 55. See also John C. Clemmons et al., "Unique and Combined Contributions of Multiple Child Abuse Types and Abuse Severity to Adult Trauma Symptomatology," *Child Maltreatment* 12, no. 2 (2007): 172; and Sheryn T. Scott, "Multiple Traumatic Experiences and the Development of Posttraumatic Stress Disorder," *Journal of Interpersonal Violence* 22, no. 7 (2007): 932.

child victimization, recognizing both risks of isolation and group contagion does not necessarily make our immediate decisions any easier.

Environment: A Contributing Factor

The *Wetiko*: In the ancient stories, and the written and oral accounts of the *wetiko*, the *wetiko* appears, or a person transforms into a *wetiko*, only in the wintertime. In some of the very old stories, a *wetiko* brings winter in the middle of the summer. During my interviews, no one could recall a case of someone becoming a *wetiko* in the other seasons. The process of becoming a *wetiko* might take a winter season.[117] One elder speculated there are fewer *wetikos* today because it is warmer than it used to be.[118] In an old story, a duck "with summer on its feet" kills the *wetiko* giant by melting its ice heart,[119] and Nelson reported that *wetikos* "sometimes, indeed frequently, recover with the warm weather, for the sun then animates all nature!!!"[120] In some stories, the *wetiko* is fine in the summer, he "lived the same as others, but in the winter he killed and ate [people]."[121] In one case, this theory leads a group to decide that a boy who had helped his mother kill his entire family, then killed her, without showing any remorse, should be killed in the summer. They made this decision even though he was helping out and acting normally at that time, because they "were afraid that if he lived through the summer he would become worse again in the winter" when it would be harder to kill him.[122]

Child Victimization: One person in the interviews explicitly linked the environmental element in *wetiko* incidents to child sexual victimization, where it is generally accepted that multiple factors must be present for an incident to occur, one of which is the environment in which the offender and victim exist.[123] David Finkelhor proposes a framework for preventing child victimization that includes instigation, selection, and protection, which can be divided into two levels: the victims themselves

---

117 Interview 4.
118 Interview 1.
119 Norman, *Where the Chill Came From*, 43.
120 Brown and Brightman, *Orders of the Dreamed*, 94.
121 Teicher, "Windigo Psychosis," 23.
122 Ibid., 57.
123 Interview 4. See the discussion of environment in Wild and Anderson, *Ampe Akely-ernemane Meke Mekarle*, s. 6.4: "The immediate environment is more than a passive backdrop against which action is played out; it plays a fundamental role in initiating and shaping that action."

and "the environments in which victims live and interact."[124] There are certain environments that tend to increase the chance of children suffering multiple victimizations.[125] It is also possible that some people, particularly youth who may have been involved in group contagion, can, like the *wetiko*s who recovered in the summer, also recover and be safe in a new, healthier environment. However, the fact some people were fine through the summer, but got worse in the winter again also indicates that a period of good behaviour in a different environment did not make everyone forget the potential for harm. Just because they do not offend in a different environment does automatically mean they will be safe once they return to their original environment.

*Wetiko*s and Child Victimization: On All Fours?

In this chapter I talked about the thinking or theories about a *wetiko*'s tactics, characteristics, and possible causes. After each description, I then talked about current thinking or theories regarding offenders and child victimization. I showed the analogies I see between these two lines of thought. In some cases, I added lessons and understandings about child victimization that I learned from the analogous theories about the *wetiko*. I see the thinking about *wetiko*s as very similar to the thinking about child victimization.

In the common law, when two cases are very similar, a lawyer might say that they are "on all fours" with each other. When two cases are so similar that they are on "all fours," the argument that follows is that the legal principles from one should be applied to the other. I argue that the thinking about the *wetiko* and about offenders and child victimization are "on all fours" with each other. Therefore, I wonder if the *wetiko* principles could be usefully applied to the present urgent issue of child victimization. If they can, this may be a powerful internal resource for communities today. In the next chapter, I will talk about these legal principles.

---

124 Finkelhor, *Childhood Victimization*, 63. At an environmental level, the "main components of the protection web … are the qualities of supervision and social connectedness."

125 See Wild and Anderson *Ampe Akelyernemane Meke Mekarle*, s. 6.3, identifying environmental factors that increase the potential for child neglect or victimization, including "high crime rates, poverty, unemployment, substance abuse, poor housing and under-resourced education system." See Finkelhor, *Childhood Victimization*, 50, for a description of high-risk environments. For example, risk increases with "a high concentration of youth in the neighborhood and the existence of a large number of youth from single-parent families." See also 58 and 73, where Finkelhor discusses risks and "buffers."

Chapter 4

The *Wetiko* Legal Principles: Response Principles, Problem-Solving Processes, Obligations, and Rights

Because there are striking similarities between the thinking around *wetiko* and child victimization dynamics, I believe the *wetiko* legal principles may be useful tools for thinking about how to protect our children from terrible harms caused by people close to us, and thinking about how to recognize and respond to people close to us who may cause terrible harm to others. This chapter will explain the *wetiko* legal principles about people's legal obligations and rights, and legal principles about legal processes for deciding and applying these obligations and rights. These principles will address how people help the person who became *wetiko*, how they protect those around the *wetiko*, how decisions to take action are reached and by whom. In the real, everyday life of any legal order, it is difficult to separate legal principles into pure rights and obligations or pure processes. However, I am going to do so here for the sake of *analytical clarity*. Basically, analytical clarity results when we organize things in a way that lets us think them through in a clearer way. Of course, it is not real life, because real life is always messier than categories or lists, but it gives us a starting point for thinking through the messiness.

I will start by outlining the legal principles about legal processes. I will then talk about legal principles about individuals' obligations and rights and will end with some general underlying principles that may be useful for thinking about the future directions of *wetiko* law. When I state a legal principle, I follow the basic rule with different examples of how it was applied to different circumstances, as well as any exceptions to it. This reminds us that legal principles are not rigid and unthinking rules. Legal rules can never fully capture all of life and experience.[1] Real life and experience may lead us to change rules, or make certain exceptions to them. Even if we don't change the rules themselves, we always decide what the rule means and whether or how to apply it in certain circumstances on the basis of our experience, resources, and situation. This is why some legal theorists argue law is more about *thinking with* rules to solve a problem than about blindly obeying them.

Wetiko **Legal Processes**

Legal processes tell us *how* legal issues are decided and *who* has the final say. Every legal order must have certain processes so that most people will accept that decision, even if they personally disagree. These processes ensure collective decisions are seen as legitimate and authoritative within the group. In the *wetiko* cases, (1) legitimate decisions are collective and open; (2) authoritative final decision-makers are leaders, medicine people, and the closest family members of the *wetiko*; and (3) there are procedural steps to determine legitimate and effective responses.

Legitimate Decision-Making Is Collective and Open

The most consistent principle in *wetiko* legal processes is that decisions regarding the *wetiko* must be made openly by the collective in order to be seen as legitimate. Borrows explains this in the context of an Anishinabek council's decision to execute a *wetiko* who had become increasingly dangerous to himself and others: "When it became clear that he was not getting any better and that his threats were becoming a matter of life and death, they went to council together rather than take action individually. This is an important Anishinabek legal principle. Their method of making judgments was collective, not individualized. They relied upon one another's viewpoints. They were deliberative. They clearly felt that the method of deciding was very important because they travelled through heavy snow to meet together."[2]

---

1 As Webber puts it, "Our statements of norms never exhaust the capacity for learning from reflection upon experience. Jeremy Webber, "The Grammar of Customary Law," *McGill Law Journal* 54, no. 4 (2009): 586.

2 John Borrows, *Canada's Indigenous Constitution* (Toronto: University of Toronto Press, 2010), 114.

This principle is often *implicit* in stories and accounts. In other words, making decisions about a *wetiko* as a group is often described as just something people *do*. In the overwhelming majority of cases that end in an execution, a group is involved in making the decision to act.[3]

At times, someone states this principle explicitly, as when describing a decision to white people. In the account Borrows relates, it is explained clearly that the execution was an "act of council." The group "formed a council to determine how to act" and that the person who performed the execution "carried into effect the determination of the council."[4] In other cases, there are indications that deliberation and persuasion took place in order for someone to agree to be the one to actually execute the *wetiko*. For example, in the case of Napanin, the group asks a medicine man to kill the *wetiko*, but he is "very unwilling and at first refused. At length, on their repeated solicitations and the conviction that otherwise ... he would destroy them, he struck him on the head with his axe."[5]

Two cases strongly suggest that, in the past, when an individual killed someone because they claimed he or she was a *wetiko*, secretly and without group input, this drastic course of action was considered suspect or illegitimate by the group. In one recorded case, an older chief, who was reported being once an excellent fur hunter, with great influence, "'caused' his son to be strangled," apparently because he feared he was becoming a *wetiko*. The recorder notes the *"apparent secrecy surrounding the death of his son seems to have forfeited [him] – his hunting luck and so his influence as a chief."* At the time the account was written, the writer says the man seems "completely finished both as an individual and as a chief," he "suffered a fate worse than death – his reputation as a

---

3 See Candice Savage, ed., *The World of Wetiko: Tales from the Woodland Cree, as Told by Marie Merasty* (Saskatoon, SK: Saskatchewan Indian Cultural College, 1974), 5; Howard Norman, *Where the Chill Came From: Cree Windigo Tales and Journeys* (San Francisco: North Point, 1982), 108; Morton Teicher, "Windigo Psychosis: A Study of a Relationship between Belief and Behavior among the Indians of Northeastern Canada," in *Proceedings of the 1960 Annual Spring Meeting of the American Ethnological Society,* ed. Verne F. Ray (Seattle: University of Washington Press, 1960), 35, 45, 53, 56, 81, and 82; Jennifer S.H. Brown and Robert Brightman, *The Orders of the Dreamed: George Nelson on Cree and Northern Ojibwa Religion and Myth, 1823* (Winnipeg: University of Manitoba Press, 1990), 89 and 92; Carlson, "Appendix Cases," 128 and 181; and Thomas Fiddler and James R. Stevens, *Killing the Shaman* (Newcastle ON: Penumbra, 1991), 88.

4 Borrows, *Canada's Indigenous Constitution,* 113.

5 Carlson, "Appendix Cases," 128. For similar reluctance to be the one to perform the execution, see 102; and Teicher, "Windigo Psychosis," 89.

hunter had vanished, and though he continued to live it was no longer as chieftain of his band."[6]

One interviewee described an incident a long time ago, when a man told the community he had killed his son because the son had become a *wetiko*. There was a lot of suspicion, unrest, and disapproval in this case, because it was done in secret, away from the group.[7] Exceptions to this general principle are found in old stories where a *wetiko* is stalking an isolated family,[8] when a child is with the *wetiko* and needs immediate rescue,[9] or where a person deliberately leads a *wetiko* to a medicine person.[10] While the first exception can be seen as obvious self-defence, I wonder if the other two can be seen as a balancing against legal principles about obligations to help and protect the vulnerable and the authority or medicine people as decision-makers, as we shall see later on.[11]

Authoritative Final Decision-Makers Are Leaders, Medicine People, and Family Members

In the historical cases of execution, there were usually specific final decision-makers. These are usually leaders, medicine people, and/ or the closest family members of the *wetiko*. In the Fiddler case, the chief of the Sucker Clan, Joseph Fiddler, and his brother, Jack Fiddler, a powerful spiritual leader, or *ogema*, were charged with murder by Canadian government officials after they executed a woman who was sick and suffering, and who they deemed at risk of becoming a *wetiko*. In this case, in the Canadian trial of the *ogema*, one witness, Angus Rae, testifies that members of the band are "bound to obey the ogema, bound to do what the ogema says."[12] While in jail, Joseph Fiddler writes a letter to the minister of justice, pleading for his life: "I was the chief of my tribe, we had much sickness, and the sick ones

---

6 Mistassini Report 1839–40, in Teicher, "Windigo Psychosis," 78. Emphasis mine.

7 Interview 4: Interview of anonymous community leader, 13 June 2009, Alberta. It was at this point, he said, that a missionary told the people they should no longer kill *wetiko*s, but instead bring them to the police to deal with.

8 See Savage, *World of Wetiko*, 7 and 10–11.

9 See Teicher, "Windigo Psychosis," 55.

10 See Savage, *World of Wetiko*, 11.

11 Regardless, some fact-finding method must have existed to determine whether a specific incident was illegitimate and suspect, or a valid exception to the rule. This is an area for future research.

12 Fiddler and Stevens, *Killing the Shaman*, 93.

were getting bad spirits and their friends were afraid of them and sent for me to strangle them … It has always been the rule of our people to strangle sick ones who went mad. No one but the chief of the tribe or one named by him could strangle anyone."[13]

Medicine people were almost always, at the very least, present and involved in the decision-making.[14] This may have been because medicine people would be in the best position to decide whether healing was possible and what measures were sufficient to ensure group safety. In one interview, an elder who practises traditional medicine and her husband observed a woman for years, but her mother and husband supervised her adequately so others were safe.[15]

In many cases, the *wetiko*'s closest relative or friend made the final decision or performed the actual act of execution. In the case Borrows relates, the reasoning is explicit: once it was "unanimously agreed that he must die," his "most intimate friend undertook to shoot him *not wishing any other hand to do it*."[16] In other cases, the people who make the final decision or actually kill the *wetiko* are the *wetiko*'s daughter,[17] companion,[18] father,[19] "closest uncle,"[20] brother,[21] husband, and son-in-law.[22]

In the case of Napanin above, where the group convinced the medicine man to kill the *wetiko*, "his own father advocated him being put to death."[23] However, this case raises an interesting question about this principle: what if two of the closest relatives disagreed? After his death, Napanin's wife was very upset and told a missionary "that he did not become dangerous"[24] and that she "did not know that he was to be killed and went to a neighbour's house with her baby." When she went to check the house where he was being kept, she saw blood, but was

---

13 Ibid., 115.
14 See the cases of Moostoos, in Teicher, "Windigo Psychosis," 93–103; and Carlson, "Appendix Cases," 154–81; and the cases of Napanin and Fiddler in Fiddler and Stevens, *Killing the Shaman*, 127 and 88 respectively.
15 Interview 1: Interview of two anonymous elders, 11 April 2009, Alberta.
16 Borrows, *Canada's Indigenous Constitution*, 112. Emphasis mine.
17 Savage, *World of Wetiko*, 6.
18 Ibid., 11.
19 Teicher, "Windigo Psychosis," 47.
20 Ibid., 56.
21 Brown and Brightman, *Orders of the Dreamed*, 89.
22 Carlson, "Appendix Cases," 102.
23 Ibid., 128.
24 Ibid., 125.

"shoved away and the door shut."[25] In this case, it is clear the father's decision was counted. It is not clear if Napanin's wife's decision was discounted or if she changed it after the fact.

If one assumes she was in disagreement or not consulted, this raises the question of why his opinion was followed over hers. What were the legal procedures and criteria used for such a decision?[26] Alternatively, did the group fail to follow proper legal processes, because of the political pressures of the time?[27] Or did Napanin's wife fail to fulfil her legal obligation towards others, by denying the danger he posed?[28] Were there ways to resolve such issues after the fact that did not take place because she left immediately afterwards?[29] While these issues raise important questions for further research, there does seem to be enough information to confirm that close relatives played an important decision-making role, along with medicine people and leaders.

There Are Procedural Steps for Determining Legitimate and Effective Responses to a Wetiko

Procedural steps include (1) recognizing and sharing information about warning signs, (2) observation, questioning, and evidence gathering to determine whether an individual fits in the *wetiko* category, and (3) determining response.

---

25 Ibid. She may later have described this incident as a murder in her Metis scrip application. See ibid., 136.

26 Because many people have more than one "closest" relative, this is an obvious question for further research.

27 Apparently, at this time, a Saulteaux prophecy that a *wetiko* was coming had "created a general terror and uneasiness" in the area (Carlson, "Appendix Cases," 127). When the group is persuading the medicine man, part of their reasoning that he would destroy them all is that he was the "predicted cannibal" (128). The fear from this could have induced the men to cut corners and fail to follow legitimate legal processes, which may have either led to a different decision, or made the decision more legitimate for Napanin's wife.

28 While Napanin's wife later said he was not dangerous after the fact, others reported he was "dangerous at intervals," and she herself told people he had begun to "act strangely" on their trip there (Carlson, "Appendix Cases," 125). Throughout the trip, he continued to "act strangely in intervals, and at such times his wife for her own safety induced him to go ahead" (134). One report says, "The poor woman sat up all night not daring to lie down lest he should kill the children or her" (127). If this was the case, it is hard to believe she was not aware of the threat he posed to others, particularly if he was escalating.

29 Napanin's wife immediately left with her children with the missionary, Rev. George Holmes, to return to Wabasca (Carlson, "Appendix Cases," 128). In the Borrows

RECOGNIZING WARNING SIGNS

In the written stories and accounts, there were certain behavioural and physical signs that, together or separate, indicate a family or group should be suspicious or cautious that a visitor might be a *wetiko*. In several cases, the first suspicious sign someone is a *wetiko* is arriving alone.[30] For example, people are first suspicious when Swiftrunner arrives without his wife and children.[31] In another recorded case, the physical signs of a horrible stink and a "haggard, wild and distressed" appearance raise suspicion and merit closer observation.[32]

When a family is alone, observing someone approaching secretively rather than openly raises suspicion. For example, in one story, an old woman sees a father and his daughter alone without the rest of the family she knew. She takes precautions (ice around her lodge), and her suspicions are confirmed when she sees the daughter "advancing cautiously," looking and listening to see if she was asleep.[33] In another story, children tell their blind grandmother they see a man swimming towards them, hiding behind reeds. The grandmother grabs an axe for protection and explains, "A sane person would not be crossing the river holding reeds in front of him and in such cold water … This is not a kindhearted one … not a kindhearted one who has come to pay us a call. He is not sane."[34]

In the interviews for this project, elders explained several "supernatural" signs that indicate a *wetiko* is coming or someone is becoming a *wetiko*.[35] Signs include seeing a dark red cow or bull, seeing a huge

---

account, the reporter says the father is "*now* perfectly satisfied." This might suggest he did not agree at the time. However, he was reported presently satisfied after the person "who carried into effect the determination of the council" gave himself to the father to fill his son's duties, and they all "made the old man presents." Borrows, *Canada's Indigenous Constitution*, 112. Emphasis mine.

30 See Paul Kane, *Wanderings of an Artist among the Indians of North America* (London: Longman, Brown, Green, Longman and Roberts, 1859), 58–61, in Teicher, "Windigo Psychosis," 61; and J.P. Turner, *The Northwest Mounted Police* (Ottawa: King's Printer, 1950), 85.

31 Ibid., 86.

32 Brown and Brightman, *Orders of the Dreamed*, 89.

33 Kane, *Wanderings of an Artist*. In this story, the woman feigns sleep and when the girl rushes in, kills her and flees. When the father arrives, he eats his daughter.

34 Savage, *World of Wetiko*, 7.

35 Interview 1; and Interview 2: Interview of anonymous elder, 13 April 2009, Alberta.

shiny black cat, like a jaguar, or sensing spirits inside a person watching you.[36] In one case, the sign that made everyone cautious was a horse that vomited up green ice.[37] In one recorded story, a husband is alerted that *wetiko*s are stalking his family by birds.[38]

One elder also explained that some people are more sensitive to the presence of a *wetiko* spirit than others. When one of the people with this sensitivity sees such a sign or feels a *wetiko* spirit close, that person tells others. The group is then on "high alert" for a *wetiko*. This means children will be watched and kept closer to adults, and families watch each other for behavioural signs of turning into a *wetiko*.[39] Anyone can become a *wetiko*, so everyone will be on high alert. Procedurally, recognizing and alerting others to signs, whether behavioural, physical, or spiritual, leads to heightened alertness, close observation, and precautions, including gathering as a group for safety.[40]

The mere presence of these signs *never* leads to any other response on its own. For example, in the story where the horse vomits green ice, it was later that winter that a man rides up with his daughter who has become a *wetiko*.[41] In the story where a bird tells a husband to go home because *wetiko*s are stalking his wife, the children have already seen two shapes, but the mother forgot.[42] In the story where the *wetiko*s arrive alone and sneak around, the woman does not kill one until the *wetiko* girl rushes in to kill her while she feigns sleep.[43] Although certain behavioural, physical, or spiritual signs raise alertness or suspicion, no response takes place without evaluating whether a particular person fits in the *wetiko* category. One way of understanding this might be to see these signs as similar to a rebuttable presumption in the common law. Further action requires observation, questioning, and evidence gathering, usually by a group or by medicine people when available.

---

36 Interview 1.
37 Interview 3: Interview of anonymous community member, 13 April 2009, Alberta.
38 Savage, *World of Wetiko*, 10–11.
39 Thanks to Jodi Stonehouse for explaining what *high alert* likely means in behavioural terms.
40 Interview 2. In this interview the elder explained once he and his wife were in the bush, trapping, when they heard someone had seen a sign there was a *wetiko* somewhere, so they quickly packed up and moved into a larger group for safety.
41 Interview 3.
42 Savage, *World of Wetiko*, 10–11.
43 Kane, *Wanderings of an Artist*.

OBSERVATION, QUESTIONING, AND
EVIDENCE GATHERING TO DETERMINE WHETHER
SOMEONE FITS IN THE *WETIKO* CATEGORY

When suspicions are raised by physical or behavioural signs, and people are alerted, the next procedural phase is observation, questioning,
and evidence gathering.

Many of the ancient stories emphasize the effectiveness of a group
discussion to determine the truth about a transformed *wetiko* or see
through a *wetiko*'s deceptive tactics and protect people from them. For
example, in the story of the childhood fox above, it was the elders who
knew the fox being friendly with Nuneskapew was really working for
the *wetiko*.[44] In another story, one man, Misku'se, grows suspicious of a
man named Pisew after talking to two other people and realizing Pisew
has told all three of them different stories about the meat he is carrying.[45]

This theme is continued in the written accounts, when strangers or
relatives appear in a camp or settlement and claim their family starved
to death. They are carefully observed, listened to, and questioned by
the group. Sometimes a group will go back to search for evidence that
corroborates or challenges the credibility of the story. Sometimes their
condition becomes obvious under close observation. A vivid example is
found in a case where a Cree man named Pepper appears and a group
gathers to listen to his account of how all his family except the one son
with him has died. As the narrator recounts, "Not a word, not a gesture
had escaped the attentive ears and sparkling eyes of some of the men of
his tribe who arrived just as he began to speak. Never was a man more
patiently listened to; his grief, or the long pauses that counterfeited it,
were not once interrupted, except by his own wailings."[46] In this case,
despite Pepper's "plausible account," he is denounced "as a murderer
and a cannibal."[47] Later, his remaining son confirms this finding.[48]

---

44 Norman, *Where the Chill Came From*, 39.
45 Teicher, "Windigo Psychosis," 36.
46 George Back, *Narratives of the Arctic Land Expedition* (Philadelphia: E.L. Carey and
    A. Hart, 1836), 175–8, in Teicher, "Windigo Psychosis," 82. See also examples of this
    pattern of group questioning and evidence gathering, ibid., 45, 56–7 (in this case with
    spiritual assistance as well), 86 (in this case with the assistance of the NWMP as well).
    See also Brown and Brightman, *Orders of the Dreamed*, 89; and Savage, *World of Wetiko*, 2.
47 Teicher, "Windigo Psychosis," 82.
48 Ibid., 83. The account goes on: "The monster had, in truth, murdered his wife and
    children, and fed upon their reeking carcasses. That the one boy was spared was
    owing, not to pity or affection, but to the accident of them having arrived at the Fort
    when they did. Another twenty-four hours would have sealed his doom also."

In the case of the "haggard, wild and distressed woman," Nelson reports she was questioned *"as usual."* Her answers are "vague, indefinite and contradictory," so she is "observed closely" and given marrow fat to eat (occasionally a cure), and separated from the group while sleeping. Eventually, this woman is executed after attempting to bite a child and kill a man guarding her.[49] Similarly, in the case of Swiftrunner, it is reported, "Suspicion fell on him" because *"upon being questioned ... he was unable to account satisfactorily for the whereabouts of his wife and children."*[50]

While these older accounts are about people who have already become an "ideal type" *wetiko,* committing terrible crimes, the procedures of observation, questioning, and evidence gathering are also used in determining whether a person is *becoming* a *wetiko.* The criterion for determining this is observation of the *wetiko* characteristics discussed in detail in the last chapter.[51] For ease of reference, I will repeat the main categories here: observable characteristics include visible lack of self-care and self-destructiveness, expressions of sadness or of distorted and obsessive thoughts and wants.

The principles of ongoing careful observation and questioning to determine what is happening continue in the oral accounts, although the two related cases involved lying or hiding by relatives, rather than the person becoming the *wetiko.* Recall the elder who realized the translator was not translating the answers to her questions and sent the translator away until she could get her own. Only when her questions were answered openly did she and her husband feel able to use the correct medicines to help the man. Similarly, in the case related above about the woman whose husband and mother hid her condition for years, the elder and her husband continued to carefully observe the woman's behaviour in a variety of settings for years before it became clear exactly what was wrong.[52]

The possibility that people may lie about becoming a *wetiko* when they are actually not is raised twice in the written accounts and interviews. Nelson reports a story of a young man who was working for him approaching him with a worry he was becoming a *wetiko.* When Nelson asks two other men what he should do, they say, "Why do you not

---

49 Brown and Brightman, *Orders of the Dreamed,* 89.
50 Turner, *Northwest Mounted Police.* Emphasis mine.
51 See chapter 2 for a detailed description of *wetiko* characteristics.
52 Interview 1. The elders report being called by her husband yet again to help her and finally recognizing behaviours linked to becoming a *wetiko.* In this case, they identified her cocooning herself in her blankets and walking with her hands out in front of her like the hooves of a cow (see warning signs, above).

give him large draughts of your strongest spirits to drink and keep him in the room beside a large fire?" He replies he is afraid it would burn him, to which they reply, "Oh! No – if he is a real Windigo it will only do him good by driving out the ice; but if he lies to you indeed, then it certainly will injure him, but it will be good for him, and teach him for the future not to impose upon people to frighten them!"[53] Similarly, when I told Marano's story about the woman who was lost in the forest in her youth and who was still, as a "middle-aged matron," watched closely and talked about when she went off alone into the forest to one of the interviewees, his opinion was that the woman was probably just trying to scare everyone by going off alone like that.[54] These responses reinforce the need for a fact-finding phase before taking action.

On a more sombre note, Marano suggests that some historical incidents of self-identification as a *wetiko* could be seen as suicidal bids. While the stories themselves do not identify these accounts with scepticism, there are some cases of self-identified *wetiko*s killing themselves or pushing others to kill them.[55] It is fair to at least consider the possibility that people well versed in the criteria for identifying a *wetiko* and selecting the response of death could fake the symptoms. In the contemporary situation, where execution is no longer a possible response option, this consideration becomes a moot point for practical purposes. However, if Marano is correct that self-identification as a *wetiko* could, in the past, be used as a form of suicide, this may suggest something about the nature of the legal principles themselves. While Marano uses this possibility as a piece of "proof" that an actual *wetiko* psychosis did not exist, I think it is at least equally possible this can be seen as "proof" that the legal criteria for categorizing someone was a *wetiko* were clear and widely known, which actually speaks to its internal legitimacy.[56]

---

53 Brown and Brightman, *Orders of the Dreamed*, 93.

54 Interview 3.

55 See Ruth Landes, *The Ojibwa of Canada: In Cooperation and Competition among Primitive Peoples*, ed. Margaret Mead (1937), 87–126, in Teicher, "Windigo Psychosis," 54 (Anishinabek); Hudson's Bay Company Archives, B. 16/A/8, London, 63–4 (Saulteaux); and W.B. Cameron, *The War Trail of Big Bear* (Toronto: Ryerson, 1926), 88–9, in Teicher (Plains Cree). All three cases involved women. In the first case, Teicher reports Ruth Landes, in another work, states the woman's death was "an escape from melancholia" (Landes, *Ojibwa Woman*, 54n9).

56 Lon Fuller lists eight features of legal legitimacy that he argues make up the "internal morality" of law, which include the law being clear (understandable) and widely known (publicized). Lon L. Fuller, *The Morality of Law* (New Haven, CT: Yale University Press, 1964) at 39.

After all, we would not have the modern phrase "suicide by cop" if the criteria that the police consider for using deadly force were not clear and widely known in certain communities.[57]

DETERMINING RESPONSE

Once a person is categorized as a *wetiko* as a result of observation, questioning, and evidence gathering, the next stage is deciding the response. Possible responses to someone who is becoming or already a *wetiko* obviously rely on fact-finding procedures of observation and questioning to assess the efficiency of the current response and the immediate danger posed to others. The available resources and broader political considerations also play an important role in determining the best response under all the circumstances.

In the past, responses ranged from ongoing observation, intense care and kindness, questioning, offering help, alerting others, and implementing a wide range of healing measures, to temporary separation with supervision, temporary secured separation, avoidance, banishment, or even complete incapacitation (death). Typically, in both recorded and oral accounts, responses take place in phases, from the least intrusive response possible to the most intrusive response, based on an ongoing assessment of their efficiency and the safety of others. Responses are based on a balancing or blending of the response principles that follow.

Wetiko Response Principles

The dominant and over-riding principle in all accounts is one of prevention of harm and ensuring group safety. Four main response principles emerge from the stories and accounts: (1) healing, (2) supervision, (3) separation, and (4) incapacitation. To a lesser extent, an additional principle, (5) retribution, is occasionally present. Much like Western sentencing law, these principles are constantly being blended and balanced on the basis of factual and social factors. An obvious part of today's political picture is that almost all options for separation and all options for incapacitation or retribution rely on the police and courts of the Canadian legal system. I will discuss this briefly in the next section on future directions.

---

57 For a description of this form of suicidal behaviour, see Kevin Caruso, "Suicide by Cop," Suicide.org, http://www.suicide.org/suicide-by-cop.html.

Healing

The vast majority of recorded *wetiko* cases demonstrate the most conventional response to a *wetiko* has always been healing.[58] The oral accounts confirm this.[59] In the interviews, the first course of action upon realizing someone was becoming a *wetiko* was usually to offer help or take the person to someone who could heal.[60] In two cases the person was healed within the community,[61] and in three cases the person was taken hours on horseback to someone with medicine who could heal. A variety of healing means were reported, including medicines, smudging,[62] and shaking "houses."[63] Cautions were that people should not try to heal someone beyond their ability and that no one has ever been completely healed.[64]

In the old stories, even the giant *wetiko*s were occasionally transformed into helpful members of a family by intense kindness and hospitality. In two very similar stories, a giant *wetiko* coming to eat a family is won over by the mother pretending to welcome him as her father.[65] In one, the giant becomes "very useful" and "a good man."[66] In the other, the giant is described as becoming "truly gentle" and continues to be "really kind" to everyone.[67] However, in two other stories, this response doesn't work. In one, after this worked with one *wetiko*, the mother tries

---

58 Robert Brightman, "The Windigo in the Material World," *Ethnohistory* 35, no. 4 (1988): 358.

59 Interviews 1, 2, and 4. In Interview 1, after reading the Borrows account in the information package, at first Carol, my translator, did not think anyone had ever been killed among the Cree in the area, as she had heard only stories of cures. Her father corrected her, saying that there were some rare incidents where death was the only option.

60 Interviews 1, 2, 3, and 4.

61 Interview 1.

62 Ibid.

63 Interview 2. This sounded like what is usually described as a "shaking tent."

64 Interview 1.

65 Teicher, "Windigo Psychosis," 22–3 and 28.

66 Ibid., 23. At the end of the story, he saves them from a bad giant and kills the bad giant. This is "why people don't kill to eat each other today."

67 Ibid., 30. In the end, he goes away to fight a windigo woman, and warns the woman not to eat the musk glands of the beaver or he will return. She hears them fighting, and, as he instructs her, tells them to stay away, off the island where people live. This is why windigos live over "there" rather than here. Otherwise they would have eaten everyone here.

it again, "apprehending no danger." She is promptly eaten.[68] In another, a family lets a *wetiko* live with them and eventually marry their daughter. Although he had been good, as winter came "when they would be sleeping at night he'd bite the daughter and she would shout and they knew that he was going to eat her, so they killed him while he slept."[69]

In the other recorded stories, people who were becoming *wetiko*s as a result of a curse were cured through "tender nursing" by a wife,[70] through medicine, care, and spiritual fight against the shaman by a mother,[71] and through a grandmother preparing a special food of dried duck, fat, and wild rice for a girl.[72] In one case, the council denounces a father for failing to call a medicine man before it was too late for healing.[73] When Nelson describes people's response to someone becoming a *wetiko*, he says, "They are in general kind and extremely indulgent to those thus infected: they seem to consider it as an infliction [affliction?] and are desirous of doing all they can to assist."[74] He also points out, "There are however, many exceptions: but these again depend upon the circumstances attending them."[75] Even in cases that end in an execution, there is usually first a step of attempted cure.[76] As Nelson's observation suggests, even if the preferred response principle is healing, the group still must evaluate all the circumstances in order to make a decision.

---

68 Ibid., 39–41 (a Montagnais Naskapi story). They had only a little bit of moose-meat in the lodge, and this *wetiko*, disappointed, threw their lodge to the wind, grabbed her, and, taking no notice of her cries and entreaties, "tore out her entrails and taking her body at one mouthful, started off without noticing the boy."

69 Ibid., 23.

70 Ibid., 59.

71 Ibid., 58.

72 Ibid., 75. The grandmother said, "If you can manage to eat the food I set before you, you will be different, everything will leave you. If you can't, you will not live, that's for sure." The girl "ate the food and then it was as though she woke up. In two days she was recovered and restored to her usual self."

73 Ibid., 46.

74 Brown and Brightman, *Orders of the Dreamed*, 95.

75 Ibid.

76 See, for example, the case of Moostoos, where a shaking tent is tried first, in ibid., 93–103; Carlson, "Appendix Cases," 154–81; and the case of Napanin, where a medicine man is called and they attempt to cure him for twenty days, with, among other things, heated bear grease, according to Bernard Cardinal, interview, in Carlson at 133. But see the case of Marie Coutreille, where there is no indication any healing methods were tried. PAA Acc: 79.266/126 Box 1, Edmonton Supreme Court Files: "Regina vs Michel and Cecil Courtreille"; and "Supreme Court," *Edmonton Bulletin*, 22 October 1887.

Supervision

In many cases, people turning into or suspected of being *wetiko*s are supervised closely, with coercion where necessary. Before, during, and after healing attempts, some degree of supervision of the *wetiko* is generally required in order to ensure the safety of people nearby. In one of the older oral accounts, a woman becoming a *wetiko* is brought in from the bush by her father, who emerges from the bush riding behind her, holding a rifle to her head, in case she tries to do anything to her two children, who are riding with her on her horse.[77] In a recorded case, a man "sprang forward to seize one of his own children" and his wife said, "Keep quiet, thou dog for if a Gun hath no effect on thee, my axe shall – I shall chop up into slices: thou hadst then better be quiet." This kept him indeed quiet for some time.[78]

In the old story of the childhood fox, the elders supervise both the deceptive fox and the intended victim.[79] In the cases where a stranger is suspected of being a *wetiko*, they are often supervised closely. In one case, after a woman arrives with many physical and behavioural signs, and attempts to bite a child, she is surrounded by men in a separate hut while she supposedly sleeps.[80] In another case, Marie Courtreille tells her husband she is going to eat him and asks to be killed. She acts strangely and hunts for weapons when she thinks her husband and stepson are asleep, "but she thought that she was watched she would throw herself down."[81] Her husband and son-in-law supervise her constantly, taking turns, and her husband does not sleep for fifteen days.[82] In the Napanin case, as Napanin becomes increasingly violent and uncontrollable, he is supervised in a separate shack for days, while they attempt to heal him, before his father decides they can no longer restrain him.[83]

Sometimes more drastic measures are required when supervision is insufficient to ensure group safety. However, careful observation

---

77 Interview 3.
78 Brown and Brightman, *Orders of the Dreamed*, 95. Nelson comments, "How they are now I cannot say, not having heard of them from the beginning of December (now April 20th)."
79 Norman, *Where the Chill Came From*, 36–9.
80 Brown and Brightman, *Orders of the Dreamed*, 89.
81 Carlson, "Appendix Cases," 102.
82 Ibid.
83 Ibid., 133.

continues, even in the cases where someone is healed. Because being a *wetiko* is considered a lifelong condition and people cannot be completely healed, some level of supervision often continues even after healing. J.D. Kohl explains that a suspected or discovered *wetiko* was "obliged to be very cautious … for some time."[84] Marano gives the case of a woman suspected of being a *wetiko* in her youth, who is still talked about and watched closely whenever she goes off alone into the forest, although at that point she is "a middle aged matron."[85] One elder said that observation and "taking care" of someone who became a *wetiko* lasts an entire lifetime, with particular attention paid at the beginning of winter. In one case, the woman who had been healed still had a couple of "relapses" where several men guarded her away from other people, bringing her back whenever she ran away, for the duration of the relapse.[86]

Separation

Many of the above supervision examples also involve a time of separation from the group, or at least from the vulnerable. Clearly, separation can be a temporary response. Sometimes it occurred while the *wetiko* was being cured. When Sioux Woman began becoming a *wetiko* as a result of a shaman's curse, "all the children were taken away, and some of the grown people went away too" while her mother attempted to cure her. "Only a few stayed there to watch her." When her mother cured Sioux Woman, "her grandchildren all came home, and they lived happily after that."[87] Sometimes temporary separation was even self-initiated. A superintendent of Indian Affairs reports a case where a man was "so well aware of his horrible propensity" that he "invariably sent his family away whenever he felt it stealing on him."[88]

Historically, depending on the circumstances, separation could also be a more permanent measure. In one case, a *wetiko* was sent away because the leader responsible for the decision did not want to kill

---

84 J.D. Kohl, *Kitchi-Gami, Wanderings round Lake Superior* (London: Chapman and Hall, 1860), 355–6, in Teicher, "Windigo Psychosis," 51.

85 Marano et al., "Windigo Psychosis," 387.

86 Interview 1.

87 Teicher, "Windigo Psychosis," 58.

88 Merrit Papers, T.G. Anderson to S. Lockhart, 9 September 1835, concerning affairs in Shebowenanning (note 5), ibid., 49.

him.[89] In another case, when a Cree man named Wisagun, and his son, who admitted to famine cannibalism, rejoin their tribe, "news of their deeds ... had gone before them, so they were received very coldly; and soon after Wisagun pitched his tent, they all, with one accord, removed to another place, as though it were impossible to live happily under the shadows of the same trees."[90]

Other white people commented on Indigenous individuals they knew or traded with who were completely avoided or shunned by all other Indigenous people. One account comments on an "ordinary half-breed hunter" who was considered to be a *wetiko*. The writer says the "only remarkable thing about him was that he was avoided by his fellows. The Indians were polite enough to him and did not appear to bear him any animosity, yet when he turned up at the post, the store emptied itself of Indians. He never hunted with an Indian family, and his trapping companions were always whites or half-breeds who had adopted the white man's ways."[91]

This separation was enforced when necessary. In another avoidance account,[92] the avoided woman "tried to join a band this winter but they refused to let her stay and threatened to kill her if she attempted to do so."[93] In the case of Wisagun, above, Wisagun follows the group and threatens them. At this point, two hunters pursue him and shoot him.[94]

Incapacitation

Historically, when healing, supervision, and separation were not enough to ensure group safety, measures for temporarily or permanently incapacitating the *wetiko* took place. Both Marie Courtreille and Napanin were tied up or restrained as they became increasingly violent

---

89 Norman, *Where the Chill Came From*, 7, quoting Cree elder John Rains: "And Hoyt's father, who was a leader there, had to make a decision about this. Because others wanted to kill this man but Hoyt's father didn't. He wanted to send him away. Someone told him, 'It will get worse and he will come back for us.' But Hoyt's father sent the man away."

90 Robert M. Ballantyne, *Hudson's Bay* (Edinburgh: William Blackwood and Sons, 1848), 50–5, in Teicher, "Windigo Psychosis," 90–2.

91 J.A. Burgesse, *Windigo*, Beaver, Outfit 277 (1947), 4–5, in Teicher, "Windigo Psychosis," 105.

92 PAA acc. 70.387, file A 280/1a, box 52, in Carlson, "Appendix Cases," 111. In this case, a woman who had survived a famine by eating those who starved to death is described as being "something like Cain, regarded with mingled feelings of fear, dislike, or superstition by her fellow Indians."

93 PAA acc. 70.387, file A 280/1a, box 52, ibid., 111.

94 Teicher, "Windigo Psychosis," 90–2.

and uncontrollable.[95] In another case, when a Cree man named Wiska-hoo drinks "grog," he always starts talking about becoming a *wetiko*. "When he had said this a few times, one of the men used to tie him slightly, and he soon became quiet; these sad thoughts at times came upon him, from the dreadful distress he has suffered; and at times took him in his tent, when he always allowed himself to be tied during this sad mood, which did not last long."[96] This goes on for three years before other measures become necessary.[97]

In the past, when no other options were available, and temporary incapacitation was no longer sufficient for securing group safety, permanent incapacitation did take place, in the form of execution. Teicher argues that "execution was not a vengeful act; it was a preventative act based on the belief that cannibalism was compulsive behavior."[98] The stated reasons for execution in the *vast* majority of cases demonstrate this principle.[99] There are several recorded accounts of this occurring, because it was the *wetiko* executions, rather than other responses, that most often came to the attention of white people. This is because they were significant events and were talked about openly among Indigenous people meeting at trading posts.[100] This is also because Canadian government officials were disturbed by these occurrences and wanted to stop them for political reasons.[101]

Several Indigenous people who executed a *wetiko* were charged with murder and in turn executed themselves (or jailed, where many died of consumption) under the Canadian legal system.[102] Even in cases where people were not arrested, the fear remained. For

---

95 Carlson, "Appendix Cases," 102 and 133.

96 Teicher, "Windigo Psychosis," 81.

97 Ibid., 81.

98 Ibid., 49.

99 See Fiddler and Stevens, *Killing the Shaman*, 94, where Angus Rae testifies, "Wasakapeequay was destroyed to protect the people"; and Carlson, "Appendix Cases," 125, in the case of Napanin, where it was explained that the killing was "justified on the ground that unless he was killed he would have killed others, and that is the custom of the country." See also Interview 1, where an elder asks his daughter, who didn't believe executions occurred, what she would do – let the *wetiko* kill her family or kill the *wetiko*?

100 See Sidney L. Harring, "The Enforcement of the Extreme Penalty: Canadian Law and the Ojibwa-Cree Spirit World," in *White Man's Law: Native People in Nineteenth-Century Canadian Jurisprudence*, ed. Sidney L. Harring (Toronto: University of Toronto Press, 1998), 237.

101 See generally, ibid.

102 See generally, ibid.

example, in the case of Napanin, the elderly medicine man who was convinced to perform the execution by the group, lived in "constant fear of being apprehended and committed for trial."[103] The government also issued warnings and proclamations that no more *wetiko* killings were allowed to occur.[104] This political situation ended execution as an incapacitation option. Once death became a possible risk of performing an execution for the executioners, regardless of who the person was, how legitimate the decision was seen by the group, or how dangerous the *wetiko* was becoming, people must have found themselves in a terrifying dilemma: they could be "dead if they did, dead if they didn't."

At this point, the only methods of incapacitation that do not carry the risk of criminal charges in the Canadian legal system are calling in police and intervention by mental health services or the Canadian justice system.

Retribution

While the vast majority of *wetiko* executions were explicitly about incapacitation to prevent future or further harm, there is a small line of past stories where death is clearly retribution. Basil Johnston describes an old story that includes a man who, after a giant *wetiko* kills his entire community, has had "only one thing to live for: revenge." He tracks the *wetiko* for hundreds of miles and kills him "in the same way the monster killed his victims – unmercifully. With utter indifference to his cries for mercy or of fear and pain, he clubbed the Weendigo to death, leaving its remains to the ravens or whoever craved the flesh of a cannibal."[105]

In one case, where the daughter of a *wetiko* does not warn the father, another sister is clear both her mother (the *wetiko*) and her sister (who didn't stop her) had angered her, especially for killing her father.[106] There is also a brief account in which J.D. Kohl describes a *wetiko* who had killed his wife and another girl, who was "regularly hunted down, so people said, and would soon receive a vengeful bullet from society."[107] Teicher argues this is a "culture bound" view of Kohls, and it

---

103 *Edmonton Bulletin*, 18 March 1897, in Carlson, "Appendix Cases," 130.
104 Ibid.
105 Basil Johnston, *The Manitous: The Supernatural World of the Ojibway* (Toronto: Key Porter Books, 1995), 227.
106 Savage, *World of Wetiko*, 6.

was just as likely the man was hunted as a preventive measure.[108] It is just as likely there was a little of both principles at play.

Wetiko Legal Obligations

Some legal obligations are apparent in the above discussions of *wetiko* legal processes, and, to avoid repetition, I will refer the reader to the place where it is previously discussed. Some legal obligations need more fleshing out, and I will do so here.

Responsibility to Help and Protect

The most consistent principle about legal obligations is that there is an obligation to help when possible and to protect the vulnerable from a *wetiko*. This responsibility is linked to the ability of the person in question. Where there is no ability to help or stop a *wetiko*, there is no expectation to do so. However, those who are able to protect others are expected to do so.

The pervasive and unquestionable nature of this obligation came across strongly in my interview with an elder who practises traditional medicine. She told a story of when she and her husband were busy trying to go on a vacation, and her sister phoned to tell them she was going to help with a man being brought down from another community for healing. The elder told her sister it sounded too dangerous to handle on her own, and her sister got mad and hung up, saying she could handle it. However, once the man arrived and she saw what was happening, she phoned back and asked for immediate help. The elder then delayed her trip to help. Throughout the interview, it was simply unimaginable that she and her husband would not help those who asked, or offer help to those they sensed might be becoming a *wetiko*. They simply did help, every time.[109]

---

107 Teicher, "Windigo Psychosis," 50, discussing the above quote from Kohl, *Kitchi-Gami*, 355–6.
108 Ibid., 52. He argues, "He is reading the Indian's mind with the eye of his own culture, and it might well be suggested that the motive for killing the forest-wanderer would not be revenge but rather the desire to prevent future cannibalism."
109 Interview 1.

This principle is also pervasive through the recorded stories. People who cannot overpower a *wetiko* seek help from those who are strong enough, either physically or through medicine. People who are strong enough always help those who are vulnerable or too weak to defend themselves. Two older stories vividly capture this. In one, two men arrive outside the tipi of an "old man known to have strong medicine powers," and the younger man signals he is normal, but his companion is "not sane." The old man realizes the young man's companion is a *wetiko* and immediately kills him. The young man then confirms he led a *wetiko* to the old man, because he knew of the old man's strong medicine powers and "wanted to see the slaughter ended."[110] In another, two men eating ducks spot a *wetiko* and one faints in fear. The other grabs him and drags him back to camp, where all the women except one elderly lady also faint. The narrator explains, "Because she did not faint, she must have had some spirit power." The two men find one man strong enough to fight the *wetiko* and the elderly lady brings him her axe to kill the *wetiko*.[111]

In many cases, the women and children go away or are taken away when people are trying to cure or fight a *wetiko*.[112] Other stories speak directly about protecting children from *wetiko*s. In one story, a *wetiko* giant takes a little boy who has wandered off and fattens him up, cutting him with a knife to see if he is fat enough to eat. When the giant and the boy travel near a group, the group asks why the boy looks like he does, and the giant replies, "I am waiting for him to get fat." That night, the group asks if the boy can sleep with them, because he would get cold sleeping with the giant. The giant agrees, and "the men told the women to hurry and run away from the place with their children for they were going to kill the giant." They do kill the giant, and "got their boy back and the women came back and had no more fear of giants, and that's why there are no giants now."[113]

In the story of Kochee, Kochee's grandmother and aunt are transformed into *wetiko*s and eat everyone in their village. They keep Kochee and his little sister, wanting them to get fat enough to eat, cutting Kochee on his head to check, and eventually eating his little sister.[114] When it is almost

---

110 Savage, *World of Wetiko*, 11.
111 Ibid., 14.
112 See Teicher, "Windigo Psychosis," 58.
113 Ibid., 24.
114 Ibid., 54.

spring, they move close to some other people. "The little boy made up his mind that he would tell these people about his aunt and grandmother. Kochee ran around and tried to play with other children but every time he did, his aunt and grandmother called him back because they feared that he would tell on them before they had a chance to kill him."[115] Finally, when his aunt and grandmother send him over to the neighbours with some human meat, he warns them that his grandmother and aunt are *wetiko*s. The man comes over on the pretext of returning a gift for the gift of meat. He tells Kochee "not to go to sleep tonight, and to run out when he knew that it was safe and to hide." Meanwhile, the man and his wife work together as fast as they can to build an ice slide sloping down from the wigwam's door. When the two women come out, they both slide, one at a time, and the couple hit them on the head and kill them. Afterwards, they adopt Kochee and move to another village.[116]

These stories reinforce the importance of protecting the vulnerable. There are other significant obligations that emerge in the *wetiko* stories and accounts as well.

Responsibility to Warn

The most explicit discussion that this is a legal obligation is found where a woman kills and eats all her children except the eldest daughter, who prevents her own death only because "she could overpower her mother." She tries to protect her youngest sister until the mother tricks her into leaving her and kills her. When the father walks in the house, the daughter is silent and the mother kills him. They then go to visit another sister. The hostess's sister "went to a group of men and passed this judgment": "Kill them both. My sister has angered me for letting mother kill our family when she could have overpowered her. My mother has particularly angered me by killing my father. Don't let them escape. Kill them."[117]

The storyteller describes the elder sister's behaviour in the father incident as "unbelievable." The daughter, knowing her mother was hiding with an axe to kill her father, "should have shouted out to warn him of the danger. She should have helped him. She had been counting

---

115 Ibid., 55.
116 Ibid.
117 Savage, *World of Wetiko*, 6.

on him to take them to a relative's camp where perhaps the mother would have recovered." Instead, she says nothing.[118] Note the sister is not denounced for failing to kill her mother herself, or for being tricked into leaving her little sister unprotected. She is killed for to her failure to warn her father, which was in her power.

In another case, a man lived in Sault Ste Marie for two years. No one knew how or where he came from. At length, "some persons sent a message from Grand Portage, at the other end of the lake, that the fellow was a windigo who had devoured his mother-in-law, his wife and children and he had fled from there because people tried to shoot him."[119] This case suggests groups also have a duty to warn other groups when they were aware that someone is a *wetiko*.

During the interviews, an elder who practises traditional medicine stressed that when people saw warning signs that a *wetiko* was coming, they would "start telling everybody right away."[120] Carol, the translator, asked what her course of action would be when she found out someone was becoming a *wetiko*: "I wouldn't go to the people first and, you know, say, 'Look at the man, he's starting to be like that.' Like, out of fairness, I would go to that person first – the person that's being affected. And, I would ask them, like, 'I notice this is starting to happen. Do you need help? Or, do you want help?' Then if that person wouldn't, then she would have to go to the people."[121]

As I mentioned previously, law is not strict rules, but something people think with. The elder's matter-of-fact answer and her discussion of balancing fairness and privacy with the responsibility to warn shows how she *thinks with* this legal principle. She is not blindly following a rule, but she is thinking about what to do in a principled way.

Responsibility to Seek Help

The most explicit discussion of this as a legal obligation is found in an Anishinabek case in which the council denounces a father. In this case, a young man says he wants to eat his sister, but he is ignored because he is "a steady young man and a promising hunter." However, he repeats this again. His parents attempt to reason with him,

---

118 Ibid., 5.
119 Teicher, "Windigo Psychosis," 51.
120 Interview 1.
121 Ibid.

but he does not respond. His sister and her husband leave for another camp, and when he realizes they have gone, he says he wants to eat human flesh. Otherwise, his behaviour is "cool, calm and quiet." His family is "much grieved" because argument and questioning have no effect. The camp grows "alarmed." Finally the father "called the men to a council." The council finds the young man is a *wetiko*. "Sentence of death was passed on him, which was to be done by his father." The father "was found fault with for not having called to his assistance a Medicine Man, who ... might have driven away the evil spirit, before it was too late."[122]

In other stories, this responsibility to seek help is more implicit. The positive consequences of seeking help and the negative consequences of not seeking help are simply stated. As referred to above under the responsibility to help and protect, in every story where a person seeks help from a stronger person, it was provided. In addition, there are good reasons to believe seeking help will make things better, because of the predominant response principle of healing, and the fact that, in the vast majority of recorded and oral *wetiko* cases, people are cured or recover upon seeking help.[123] On the negative side, elders in the interviews discussed other relatives like the father in the above case, who, although they did ask for help, did not tell them the whole story,[124] and another interviewee saw becoming a *wetiko* a result of a choice not to seek help,[125] because not seeking help or not being honest about what a person needs help for makes things worse.

Responsibility to Support

Although someone who turned *wetiko* could recover for a time, oral and written sources explain he or she "could seldom be totally cured."[126] In one interview for this project, an elder who practises traditional medicine said she has never heard of a person being completely

---

122 Teicher, "Windigo Psychosis," 46.
123 Brightman, "Windigo in the Material World," 358. See also Teicher, "Windigo Psychosis," 108; and Interview 1.
124 See "Tactics," chapter 3 of this volume; and Interview 1.
125 See "Causes," chapter 3 of this volume; and Interview 4.
126 Savage, *World of Wetiko,* 1.

healed from becoming a *wetiko*.[127] Because it is a lifelong condition, they must be watched and taken care of for life. She explained that when a *wetiko* is healed, the healer is then responsible for taking care of that person for life. She gave two examples of individuals she and her husband still take care of, mainly through prayer, and especially as winter approaches. In one case, this taking care included periods of separation and observation upon observing a relapse.[128] At this point, Carol, my translator, the elder's daughter, stopped translating and asked her mother about the woman who had the relapses. This woman was still alive, but had been healed by her grandfather, who himself had passed away. "Who," Carol asked, "takes care of her now?"[129] The elder replied that she and her husband did.[130] The responsibility had been passed down to the next generation. The time span of this responsibility is striking, as is the reasoning behind it. If a *wetiko* can never be completely cured, then that person needs to be taken care of for life.[131]

Another striking obligation to support in *wetiko* stories is the responsibility to support relatives who relied on a *wetiko* when a *wetiko* was permanently incapacitated. In Borrows's account, the man who carried out the council's decision to kill the *wetiko* then gave "himself to the father of him who is no more: to hunt for him, plant and fill all the duties of a son."[132] In the case of Kochee, once his grandmother and

---

127 The reasoning behind this was that healing removes the *wetiko* spirits, and if they all are removed, then the person would have no spirit left, and would die, or, that it would be too dangerous to the medicine person to remove them all, as the *wetiko* spirit would attack him or her (Interview 1). In another interview, this same idea was explained, but as removing shards of ice, rather than spirits (Interview 4).

128 Interview 1.

129 Ibid.

130 Ibid.

131 Interestingly enough, experts increasingly recognize that, "like other compulsive behaviors, impulses to offend sexually require lifelong management." Relapse prevention programs are "adapted from addictions research and practice." See John H. Hylton, *Aboriginal Sexual Offending in Canada*, 2nd ed. (Ottawa: Ontario Aboriginal Healing Foundation, 2006), 104. http://www.ahf.ca/downloads/revisedsexualoffending_reprint.pdf. A pilot program in Ontario, "Circles of Support and Accountability," where offenders are paired with a trained volunteer who provides ongoing support and monitoring, appears to be a very effective way to prevent recidivism. See Correctional Services of Canada, "Let's Talk," http://www.csc-scc.gc.ca/text/pblct/lt-en/2006/31-3/7-eng.shtml.

132 Borrows, *Canada's Indigenous Constitution*, 112.

aunt are killed, the people who kill them adopt him and take him to another village to live with them.[133] Similarly, in the Fiddler case, L.R. MacKay, in a letter of support for Joseph Fiddler's pardon, writes, "I venture to affirm that the children of the woman so summarily disposed of have been, ere this, adopted by every mother heart in the band."[134]

Like the lifelong support for a *wetiko*, the time span of this obligation is remarkable. Unlike the support for the *wetiko*, where the responsibility clearly attaches to the healer, it is not clear how it was decided who held this responsibility in every case. In two cases, the responsibility lies with the person who incapacitated the *wetiko*. However, the practical aspects of children being adopted by "every mother heart" are not clear from MacKay's letter (understandably). More research is required to determine how this was decided.

Wetiko Legal Rights

The *wetiko* stories also show principles about legal rights – what people should be able to expect from one another. Rights almost always mean someone else has a related responsibility, some of which we have already identified. Once again, to avoid repetition, if I have already discussed this right from another angle, I will refer the reader to that place.

Few rights are absolute. Most rights must be balanced against other people's rights and responsibilities, as well as the overall needs of the group in question. This is just as likely true in Indigenous societies as it is in Canadian Charter or international law. When we talk about legal rights, we often talk about the difference between *substantive* and *procedural* rights. While there is overlap in real life, substantive rights are usually about what people should be able to expect from one another or a governing body. Procedural rights are usually about fairness in legal decision-making. The *wetiko* stories reveal procedural rights and substantive rights.

---

133 Teicher, "Windigo Psychosis," 55.
134 Fiddler and Stevens, *Killing the Shaman*, 79. MacKay goes on, "My experience covering a period of twelve years had led me to infer that the majority of Indians are actuated by more genuine love for friends and relatives than white people are."

Procedural Rights in the Wetiko *Stories*

THE RIGHT TO BE HEARD

This right attaches to a person suspected of being a *wetiko*, and, in some cases, their companions. As discussed under the procedural stage of observation, questioning, and evidence gathering, suspected *wetiko*s were always given a chance to tell their story. In one case, when a father and son arrive together, and the father is finally shot because he refuses to leave and utters threats, the boy, wounded in the arm, "offered to confess all he knew." The men all stop and listen to him.[135]

THE RIGHT TO DECIDE

This right is attached to the closest family members of a *wetiko*, and in some cases, a person in the process of becoming a *wetiko*, when drastic or irreversible measures had to be taken. As discussed under authoritative decision-makers, it appears, in most cases, the closest family member to the *wetiko* had a right to make or carry out final decisions about him or her. Clearly, this right is not absolute and would have to be balanced against the obligation to protect and the rights of other family members to decide too.

In some cases, the *wetiko* asks the family to leave when he or she feels dangerous, like the man under the principle of separation did. In some cases, the *wetiko* asks to be killed, as discussed under the observation, questioning, and fact-finding stage. In one case, a woman thought she was becoming a *wetiko*: "The people around her looked like beavers and she wanted to eat them. So she ordered her brother-in-law to straitjacket her, stun her with an axe, then set fire to her and her tent. While this was done, her husband and children looked on, for she had an undisputed right to dispose of herself as she chose."[136]

In a similar case, a middle-aged woman "felt that she was going to kill and eat her grandchildren. She asked for a rope in order to hang herself and this was provided to her. She hanged herself in the tent right before her own family." Apparently she first asked to be killed, but no one would do it. Finally, one of the men "fixed the rope for her."[137]

---

135 Teicher, "Windigo Psychosis," 83.
136 Landes, *Ojibwa Woman*.
137 Ibid., 64.

Substantive Rights

THE RIGHT TO LIFE AND SAFETY

This right is directly linked to its matching obligation, the responsibility to help and protect.

THE RIGHT TO BE HELPED

This right is attached to the *wetiko* and the family of the *wetiko*. It is directly linked to two matching obligations: the responsibility to seek help and the responsibility to help and support. Again, when the elder who practises traditional medicine was talking about the responsibility to warn, she says her *first reaction* would be to "offer that person assistance before – you know like, I could help you, I know someone who could help you – like, do you want help?"[138] Note how she offers help before she even asks if they want it. The help is there for them if they want it.

THE RIGHT TO ONGOING SUPPORT

This right is attached to the *wetiko* and those who rely on the *wetiko*. It is directly linked to the matching obligation of a responsibility to support.

General Underlying Principles

When people make legal decisions, they consider rights, obligations, and more general principles that apply in a given situation. Two underlying principles from the ancient *wetiko* stories that carry into more recent cases may help us understand the reasoning behind certain decisions and also be important practical considerations for future directions in *wetiko* law. These are (1) the principle of reciprocity – helping the helpers; and (2) the principle of efficacy – being aware and open to all effective tools and allies.

The Principle of Reciprocity: Helping the Helpers

Many of the ancient Cree and Anishinabek stories demonstrate the importance of practising reciprocity – of concretely thanking and caring for helpers against the *wetiko*.

---

138 Interview 1.

In one Anishinabek story, Nanabush meets the windigo. Nanabush is weeping and fetching a roasting stick for the windigo to impale him and cook him on when he meets a weasel. He tells the weasel he is going to die and why. The weasel says, "Nanabushu, nevertheless I will try to slay him. And as a reward to myself I shall expect some kind of blessing from you. So, therefore, if you fail to do something for me, I would not kill him." Up spoke Nanabushu: "As your reward for killing him, I will make you proud of yourself." The weasel does kill the windigo, and Nanabush wonders aloud, "How now my little brother! Wonder what I can do so that he may be very thankful! Therefore then will I paint him." He then paints the weasel with white clay, leaving a black tip on this tail, and the weasel runs around very proud. Nanabush tells him, "Therefore in this manner do I render thanks to you," and says the weasel would look like this in the winter "as long as the world lasts."[139]

In a very similar Cree story, Wesakaychak is frozen with terror and in despair when he meets a *wetiko*. His "plight was pitiful, but yet he felt he must use his wits." He tries to call the *wetiko* his brother, but the *wetiko* yells for him to hurry up and gather wood, as he had no brother. It seems hopeless, but then an ermine runs by. Weskaychak pleads with the ermine to jump down the *wetiko*'s throat and bite his heart to kill him, promising to make the ermine "the most beautiful of all creatures." Weskaychak "pleaded so earnestly the ermine took pity on him and jumped into the mouth of the *wetiko*." When Weskaychak realizes the *wetiko* is dead, he says to himself, "If it had not been for my presence of mind, I would not have been breathing now." He "tenderly" washes the blood off the ermine, and paints him with white clay, with black around his eyes and the tip of his tail. The ermine runs off, proud of its new coat. The story ends, "Ever since then, when winter comes, this little animal puts away its original colors and dons that which Weskaychak gave it as a reward for service."[140]

In many other old stories, someone who kills a *wetiko* is praised, given gifts, and taken care of afterwards. In one story, a starving weasel kills the *wetiko* and the man who asked him to do this kills a moose and gives him some of the meat.[141] In another story, after the weasel kills the *wetiko*, by chewing out his ice heart, he is freezing, and the man "quickly

---

139 Teicher, "Windigo Psychosis," 26.
140 Ibid., 34. A very similar or abbreviated version of this story, from a different source, is found at 35.
141 Norman, *Where the Chill Came From*, 31–3.

built a fire to thaw the weasel's chattering teeth."[142] A girl who turns into a weasel and kills the *wetiko* "received many praises. And some other gifts" once she was a girl again.[143] One story speaks of the consequences of responding to help with fear instead of care. A man grows scared of his two supernatural sons who killed a *wetiko*, and asks people to kill them before they grow too powerful. He is sent away and told he will have to hide in the bush, only coming out for food. The father flies out "like a bluejay" and the narrator says, "And it's true, you don't hardly ever see a bluejay flying in the open; they're always flitting in the bush."[144] An exception to this general principle is found in a story where an owl, working for the *wetiko*, is forced to work for a man and made to kill the *wetiko*. After the *wetiko* dies, the man keeps making the owl work for him, to thaw the ice on many lakes and streams.[145]

The Principle of Efficacy: Being Aware and Open to All Effective Tools and Allies

In many of the old stories, help comes from unexpected places, from both inside and outside the community, from people connected to the *wetiko*, and even tools that originally came from white people and are generally seen as (and have been) destructive forces within Indigenous societies.

Several stories tell about members of the community who might be easily overlooked as helpers. In one story, where a *wetiko* is throwing trees, a man, Anikoweste, is mad and frustrated because an old woman he asks advice from just tries to sleep and dream. In the end, when the *wetiko* arrived, the hunters had "gathered enough strength to kill it, which they did." The narrator explains, "It was a good thing the old woman threw herself to the ground so much. It was a good thing she couldn't stay away from dreaming. It helped everything."[146] In another story, an old woman is the only one willing to be the "generous one" willing to sacrifice her life "for the safety of so many," by agreeing to be bait for a trap set to kill the *wetiko*. She does a great job, and her actions save the people.[147] In another story, a little girl is

---

142 Ibid., 59–60.
143 Ibid., 72.
144 Teicher, "Windigo Psychosis," 31.
145 Norman, *Where the Chill Came From*, 92–3.
146 Ibid., 52.
147 Brown and Brightman, *Orders of the Dreamed*, 86–7.

the one who kills the *wetiko*,[148] and in yet another, a "hunchback who had been despised by the people was called upon for help against a [*wetiko*] woman who was coming to destroy the village. He spurned the gifts that were offered him, but nevertheless went to meet the [*wetiko*] woman and slew her."[149]

Help is also found outside communities. Many animals act as effective allies against *wetiko*s in the old stories. Allies include a weasel,[150] a duck (with summer on its feet),[151] an owl (who is known to cause trouble and who was suspected of causing a famine that was really caused by the *wetiko*),[152] a team effort by porcupines and a weasel,[153] a team effort by smoke and a weasel,[154] crows (who tell villagers when a windigo killed a man, and also arrive to tell the village that the *wetiko* is dead when they are scared to go out hunting),[155] snakes, who wrapped themselves around the *wetiko* and killed it,[156] a moose, who carries summer on its back to kill the *wetiko* (a frog and heron, who guard summer, decide a moose is a better runner than a deer because the deer zigzags),[157] a wolverine, who sends a man, Peyases, to his birthplace for protection while he kills the *wetiko* who is after him,[158] and a walrus, who takes two little boys fleeing from a *wetiko* across a lake to safety, then drowns the *wetiko* when the *wetiko* asks for a ride and hurts his back despite his instruction not to move.[159]

Even people close to the *wetiko* sometimes end up helping people escape from or kill the *wetiko*. In one story, it is the *wetiko*'s "kind-hearted" brother who hides a man from his giant *wetiko* brother and helps him escape to warn his village.[160] In another, a boy prisoner,

---

148 Norman, *Where the Chill Came From*, 72. She does this, first, by drinking hot tallow, which somehow weakens and hurts the *wetiko*'s heart, and second, by transforming into a weasel to crawl down his throat and bite his heart.
149 Teicher, "Windigo Psychosis," 24. Teicher relates a similar or extended version of this story, from a different source, at 26–7.
150 Norman, *Where the Chill Came From*, 32–3.
151 Ibid., 43.
152 Ibid., 55.
153 Ibid., 59.
154 Ibid., 62–3.
155 Ibid., 66.
156 Ibid., 79–80.
157 Ibid., 85–6.
158 Ibid., 89.
159 Teicher, "Windigo Psychosis," 36.
160 Ibid., 19.

whom the *wetiko* cut with a knife to see if he was fattened up enough to eat, tells villagers about the *wetiko* and they come and kill him.[161] An almost identical story occurs with a man being the prisoner who rushes over to warn a settlement.[162] In yet another, it is the *wetiko*'s wife who hides an unwitting visitor and cooperates with him to kill the giant *wetiko*.[163]

Finally, in some stories, people do use tools and methods from white people when they see them as effective weapons against a *wetiko* or for curing a *wetiko*. In one story, when the elder is conjuring, he sees a storekeeper at the Hudson Bay Company showing someone a screwdriver. He says, "We can use that!" and conjures the screwdriver to him. The men then use it to kill the *wetiko*.[164] Some medicine people saw large amounts of strong alcohol as effective for curing a *wetiko*.[165] In an HBC journal, Bill Campbell reports sending Jack Fiddler "sixteen ounces of Scotch whiskey for a cure for [a woman turning into a *wetiko* and attempting suicide]." The following summer, Jack Fiddler "told Big Bill the medicine worked well. He had poured some of it into the fire as a burnt offering for assistance from beneficient other-than-humans in the forest."[166] This suggests the origins of tools are less important than how they are used, and their efficiency in curing or stopping a *wetiko*.

While I realize people may disagree strongly, I also think this may be how some people viewed (and view) Christianity, despite many other devastating impacts from religious people. There are old stories and reported cases where people ask and receive help for or against a *wetiko* from priests and missions.[167] Conversion to Christianity and confession of sins was sometimes accepted as evidence a *wetiko* was no longer a

---

161 Ibid., 20.
162 Ibid., 21.
163 Ibid., 20.
164 Norman, *Where the Chill Came From*, 35.
165 Brown and Brightman, *Orders of the Dreamed*, 93. Reports were that "large draughts of high wines; double-distilled spirits or the spirits of wine … taken … frequently, and kept beside a large fire, flows to the heart and thaws the ice."
166 Fiddler and Stevens, *Killing the Shaman*, 53.
167 See Teicher, "Windigo Psychosis," 64; E.T.D. Chambers, *The Ouaniche and Its Canadian Environment* (New York: Harper and Brothers, 1896), 301–5, in Teicher, "Windigo Psychosis," 79; and PAA Acc. 70.387. A. 281/327, box 59; and *Edmonton Bulletin*, 15 March 1897. "Lesser Slave Lake" in Carlson, "Appendix Cases," 144–5.

threat to those around.[168] Brightman and Carlson suggest Christianity is a factor in a decrease in the *belief* in *wetikos*, and this may be so.[169] However, the one elder I interviewed who continues to practise traditional medicine, including healing people becoming *wetikos* today, *and* who is also a practising Catholic, stated her belief that there are likely fewer *wetikos* today because Christianity means fewer people practise bad medicine, and more people are protected from it.[170]

This belief is actually not at odds with a story about Jack Fiddler, who one day decides to pray to the Christian God. In front of everyone, he tells God he wants a little spoon to mix his medicine and a file to sharpen his tools. When neither appears, he gives it up for a bad job.[171] Jack Fiddler and the elder in the interviews actually have the same criteria of efficiency and usefulness of Christianity as a spiritual tool. They just reached different conclusions. It is well beyond my capacity or inclination to delve any further into this complex area. My point here is just to highlight the similar principled reasoning about new (in this case, spiritual) tools by two people who practise or practised traditional medicine and were or are called upon to help or deal with *wetikos*: when a new tool or method is helpful, they use it. When it is not, they don't.

On a similar note, despite the generally dismal failure of the Canadian justice system in relation to Indigenous people, there is evidence it was occasionally used as an effective tool for investigation and/or incapacitation. Once police were present, there are cases where Indigenous people took *wetikos* to the police to deal with.[172] The best-documented case of this is the case of Swiftrunner. While there is not enough information

---

168 Kohl, *Kitchi-Gami*, 355–6, in Teicher, "Windigo Psychosis," 39. See also the case of Veronique, a woman, who, "before her conversion to Christianity," ate the body of her husband and her three children, killing one, as well as killing and eating another woman who had eaten the body of her own child, in Chambers, *Ouaniche and Its Canadian Environment*, 301–5, in Teicher, "Windigo Psychosis," 78.

169 See Brightman, "Windigo in the Material World," 374; and Nathan D. Carlson, "Reviving Witiko (Windigo): An Ethnohistory of 'Cannibal Monsters' in the Athabasca District of Northern Alberta, 1878–1910," *Ethnohistory* 56, no. 3 (2009): 381.

170 Interview 1.

171 Fiddler and Stevens, *Killing the Shaman*, 44.

172 See *Edmonton Bulletin*, 2 March 1889, in Carlson, "Appendix Cases": "An elderly half breed woman named Paquette was brought in from Stony Plain on Thursday by her relatives and handed over to the police as insane. She was removed to Fort Saskatchewan the same evening. She is said not to have eaten anything for ten or twelve days and exhibits all the symptoms said to be shown by a person about to become a weh-ti-go."

about all the decision-making processes to be sure, this appears to be a case where Cree law and Canadian law work together harmoniously to achieve the same result.

When Swiftrunner's relatives saw warning signs, they reported their suspicions to the police. They then co-investigated for evidence. Upon discovery of boiled bones and other evidence of murder and cannibalism, as well as Swiftrunner's subsequent confession, both groups reached the decision that execution was the best response. The only difference in opinion seems to be the Cree group wanted him executed on the spot and the Canadian group insisted on jailing him until a trial, at which they sentenced him to death. He was hanged.[173] Of course, in this case, it is a reasonable assumption that the police must have been available, receptive, and trustworthy in order to be a realistic resource.

Wetiko Legal Principles: A Summary of the Findings

This is a big chapter that talks about a lot of ideas, so I am going to summarize it here before we move on to future directions in *wetiko* law and its possible application to violence and child victimization today. By analysing *wetiko* stories and accounts the same way I was taught to analyse legal cases in law school, I was able to identify many rich legal principles that, together, give us a more complete picture of this area of law. These principles are not unbending rules that everyone blindly follows or that result in the same outcome in every case. Instead, they are intellectual resources that people use to think with when they are faced with a pressing issue, like a *wetiko*.

I identified principles about *legal processes*, including the principles that legitimate decisions are collective and open, that authoritative decision-makers are leaders, medicine people, and close family members, and that legitimate responses require three procedural steps: recognizing warning signs; observation, questioning, and evidence gathering to determine whether someone fits in the *wetiko* category; and determining the response. I identified principles about *legal responses*.

---

173 Turner, *Northwest Mounted Police*, 499–501, in Teicher, "Windigo Psychosis," 85–6. On the basis of evidence found at the camps, Turner suggests the Cree group would also have executed him: "He barely escaped death, the usual penalty for such a crime, at the hands of his tribe. But it caught up with him, and imprisonment at Fort Saskatchewan was merely a prelude to his inevitable execution in the more orderly and humane manner of the white man" (86).

Responses usually go from least intrusive to most intrusive, as needed, and available resources and larger political realities affect decisions. The overall principle is ensuring group safety and protection of the vulnerable. There are four response principles that are blended and balanced, depending on the facts in a particular case. These are healing, supervision, separation, and incapacitation. To a lesser extent, retribution may also be considered.

I also identified legal principles about *obligations,* including a responsibility to help and protect, a responsibility to warn, a responsibility to seek help, and a responsibility to support. I identified legal principles about both *procedural and substantive rights.* Procedural rights include the right to be heard and the right to decide. Substantive rights include the right to life and safety, the right to be helped, and the right to ongoing support. Finally, I identified two *underlying, general principles* – the principle of reciprocity: helping the helpers; and the principle of efficacy: being aware and open to all effective tools and allies.

Together, these principles give us a clearer picture of the law that was always there in the *wetiko* stories. This is law. Distinctly and unmistakably law. If nothing else, if there is no future in broadening the application of *wetiko* law, then I hope this chapter effectively demonstrates this. I hope it shows that we can analyse oral and written stories and accounts of collective problem-solving within Indigenous societies, and start to speak to each other about the law we recognize in them. I hope seeing the law in these stories will encourage people to reject outdated stereotypes and reject lies about themselves and their ancestors. I hope both Indigenous people and white people can look at *wetiko* stories and see the enduring strength and resourcefulness in Indigenous legal traditions.

Of course, I also hope for more ...

Chapter 5

Future Directions in *Wetiko* Law: Reality, Research, and Resources

I came to *wetiko* law wanting help with a particular issue: how to respond to the violence and child victimization today in a principled and effective way. I have concluded that the *wetiko* can be seen as a legal concept, that the thinking and theorizing about *wetiko* dynamics is similar to the current thinking and theorizing about offenders and child victimization dynamics, and that there are several identifiable legal principles in the *wetiko* stories and accounts. Where do we go from here? What are possible future directions for *wetiko* law, especially in regard to my question?

Many discussions about Indigenous law are about how or if it can be harmonized with state legal systems. This cannot be ignored, but I do not think it is a good starting point. The reality is that *wetiko* law *is* being practised today. At least some people, in at least some Cree communities, think with the *wetiko* principles. They follow *wetiko* legal processes and they help some people in a principled and effective way. Borrows points out several of the *wetiko* legal principles that could still be practised today. I will add where these principles fit in my analysis for consistency. He argues we could still:

1 Wait, observe, and collect information [*a legal process principle: the procedural stages of recognizing signs and of observation, questioning, and evidence gathering*];
2 Counsel with [our] friends and neighbours when it is apparent something is wrong [*a legal process principle: legitimate decision-making is collective and open*];
3 Help the person who is threatening or causing imminent harm [*a response principle – healing; an obligation – the responsibility to help and protect; and a right – the right to help*];

4 If the person does not respond to help and becomes an imminent
   threat to individuals or the community, remove them so that they
   do not harm others ... [*a general response principle: ensuring group
   safety and protecting the vulnerable, the response principle of separation,
   the obligation to help and protect, ensuring the right to life and safety, the
   general principle of efficiency*];
5 Help those who rely on that person by restoring what might be
   taken from them by the treatment [*the obligation to support and the
   right to ongoing support*];
6 Have both the collective and the individual participate in the resto-
   ration [*the obligation to support and the right to ongoing support, and the
   general principle of reciprocity*].[1]

Between the Cree elders and Borrows's analysis, it is obvious that,
despite the ongoing presence of the Canadian legal system, some people *do* practise *wetiko* law today, and more people *could* practise it, at
least without running into Canadian legal barriers.

This means that the most logical place to begin further research is
not *wetiko* law's relationship with Canadian state law at all. Rather, the
place to begin is within Indigenous societies. There are many questions
about internal histories, practices, knowledge, interest, interpretation,
and capacity. Where are these principles still being practised today?
Where are they not, and why are they not? Do other people see value in
broadening their application to present issues of violence and victimization? What are the internal barriers? I have drawn on many different
sources across a vast amount of time and space, and from two separate
societies, the Cree and the Anishinabek, for this project. How do the
practices of *wetiko* law differ between these societies and from place to
place? What are the different histories? Where does it fit in the larger
legal traditions it is just one small part of?

There is also the issue of recognizing and accessing internal resources.
I interviewed a very small number of Cree people in northern Alberta,
three of whom are respected elders who practise traditional medicine
and most of whom (all but the two youngest) grew up living a traditional lifestyle and have Cree as a first language. There was a generation
gap in knowledge of *wetiko* law, even in these interviews. The younger

---

1 John Borrows, *Canada's Indigenous Constitution* (Toronto: University of Toronto Press,
   2010), 115.

adults I interviewed could describe the scary stories of the "ideal type" *wetiko*, but did not know any stories about people's *responses* to people becoming a *wetiko*.[2] One young adult who comes from a reserve closer to a major city had never heard of the *wetiko*.[3] Who can provide resources for learning more about *wetiko* law today? Where might we recognize these principles in play, even if they are no longer talked about as law? How do we talk across generations and diverse backgrounds? In particular, how do we bridge different understandings of "supernatural" signs and means, and how do we bridge different understandings about what law is, and where it comes from?

Of course, part of the contemporary internal reality of *wetiko* law is the surrounding political reality of Indigenous people's relationships and histories with the Canadian state and legal system. For example, for a very long time now, the response principles of separation and incapacitation require the use of police and then justice or mental health systems. If we apply the general principle of efficiency, then *if* these are useful tools or allies, using them can be seen as an application, rather than an abandonment of *wetiko* law. Unfortunately, today, in many communities, the police may not be accessible, responsive, or trustworthy, as we assume they were in the Swiftrunner case. This is a real problem. Another political reality is that the legitimacy and authority of decision-makers may be contested and divided by many factors. This can create an undercurrent of uncertainty and doubt about particular decisions.

I spent some time stating how the thinking and theorizing about the *wetiko* is analogous to the current thinking and theorizing about violence and child victimization. Where are the differences? How might these differences affect the usefulness of applying the *wetiko* legal principles to violence and victimization? Finally, whether we include child victimization under the broad legal category of *wetiko,* or apply the principles analogously, what are the practical differences in applying these principles in the current situation? For example, what further knowledge, tools, and resources would be required to apply the principle of ongoing support to a sexual offender? What does healing itself look like? How does generational poverty and overcrowded, inadequate housing

---

2 Interview 5; and Interview 6: Interview of anonymous community member, 14 June 2009, Alberta.

3 Interview 5: Interview of two anonymous young adult community members, 14 June 2009, Alberta.

affect how possible fulfilling an obligation for ongoing support to an offender's family would be if the offender needed to be separated or incapacitated for a time?

These are big questions. There is much more research and deliberation that must take place prior to applying *wetiko* legal principles more broadly to violence and victimization today. The broader application of *wetiko* law will not magically solve the complex social, political, and legal problems of today. That is not the point. This book demonstrates there are internal intellectual resources in Cree and Anishinabek societies. These resources enabled (and enable) people to think about and respond to horror and violence in principled and effective ways. The future direction of *wetiko* law will, in the end, depend on whether or not people see it as a meaningful and useful resource for the pressing issues they face today.

In the end, all I can honestly say is that *I* think *wetiko* law is a meaningful and useful resource for facing the violence and victimization in some communities. We need something that teaches us how to protect those we love, from those we love. We need something strong enough to fight a curse. Otherwise the internal violence and victimization will eat us alive. It will accomplish what the residential schools could not. I don't want this for our children. I think we need *wetiko* law today.

Beyond Sweet Dirt

Sometimes a person needs a story more than food to stay alive.[1]

Claire woke up alone by the river. There was no white dirt in the wound and there was no old woman. Her arm ached. She walked down to where she had seen the old woman digging in the bank, and sure enough, she saw the soft white dirt she had brought to her. Claire walked down to the river and washed her arm, just as the old woman had in her dream. She was going to take some of the sweet dirt, but then she stopped, as if she had just seen a future that was terrifyingly sad. With that, she threw herself back down on the ground and dreamed. The old woman was walking away with the quiet baby.

"Wait," Claire said. "Thank you, thank you Grandmother for the sweet dirt. But that's not enough. What about the *wetiko*s? What are we supposed to do about them? Because I can't just keep getting bitten. I might be bitten five more times. I might give up and start drinking to numb the pain. I might give up and wake up one morning to see my teeth marks in a child's arm. We need something more. If we can't stop the *wetiko*s, we would have to be like the ravenous people and mine the whole riverbank, and once it is all gone, it will be all gone. Then where will we be? We need something more. Something to protect us from the *wetiko*s, something to bring them back to themselves, to us, something to help us be strong together."

---

1 B.H. Lopez, *Crow and Weasel* (San Francisco: North Point, 1990), 48, as cited in John Borrows, "With or Without You: First Nations Law in Canada," *McGill Law Journal* 41 (1996): 629n84.

The grandmother stopped. She turned and sat down and thought for a very long time. Finally she spoke. "It's true," she said, "you do. What do I have? What can I give you?" Again she was silent. She thought for a very long time. Then she spoke again. "From what I remember, we can't do it alone. We will need some help for this. You go home now, and look for someone you think may want to help. I will go too, and see who might be able to help us with such things. We will meet back here in four days."

Claire went home. She didn't know how she felt. Half hopeful, half disappointed. And worried. Whom could she ask? Who might want to help? Who would dare, when for years no one had even been able to talk about what was happening when people transformed into *wetiko*s. If they did at all, it was in anguished whispers. She was sure she could not ask her family. After all, it was her father's teeth marks in her sister's leg, her sister was silent, and her mother had turned away from her. Whom could she ask?

As she passed the house of her friend Sky, she saw Sky sitting under a tree, reading a comic. Could she ask Sky? She took a deep breath, went over, and told her the whole story. Sky listened intently, and never laughed once, even though she was always laughing. As if she too, was seeing a future where she lost her cousin Claire to the *wetiko* sickness, where this terrible pain she also felt, from a bite mark on her ankle, would be passed down to the next generation. She said she would come.

Four days later, both girls walked down to the river. Would the old woman come back to meet them? Or would the dream evaporate? They sat and waited. They ate sunflower seeds and read comics, because Sky always had comics with her, and they waited. Eventually, the gentle roar of the river and the lazy heat of the day made them grow tired, and they dozed off into a perfect summer afternoon nap. The next thing they knew, they were dreaming together.

Near the river, only feet away from where they sat, they saw a most extraordinary gathering. There were chiefs in full regalia, some they recognized and some quite different. There were elders resting under trees, and people gathering and making medicines, chatting with each other and exchanging herbs and roots. There were a few white people, dressed in old-fashioned clothes, one or two even wearing old-time Jesuit and judge's robes. They were very quiet and looked a bit ill at ease. To their surprise, they recognized some of their relatives there too. They spotted a great-uncle swapping stories and medicine with another elderly man, and two great-aunts, laughing their heads off with a group of women who all seemed like old friends. And there was more. Sky was a reader and pointed out Jack Fiddler to Claire, who was telling a joke to another elderly man Sky thought might be his brother Joseph. A shaman was conjuring, a bright ball of what looked like sheer light between his fingertips. There were animals too, walking among the humans, just as the old stories and elders talked about. There were snow-white weasels with black-tipped tails. There were porcupines, owls, ducks, and a wolverine. There was even a moose and a giant walrus, who might have been having a debate about something.

The grandmother must have brought people from all over time and space. What a sight! In wonder, they stared. Then Claire spotted the old woman walking towards them. "They are here," she said. Claire couldn't think of any words, but Sky was always curious. She blurted out, "Who are they?" The grandmother smiled. "You must be Sky. What a good choice Claire."

Then she explained, "Everyone gathered has something to teach us about these things, about people we love turning into *wetikos*, about healing and protection, and how to be strong together." "But how did you do it?" Sky asked, "how did you gather them here?" The grandmother nodded approvingly. "It wasn't easy," she said. "I had to think of what might help, and I finally thought of the laws we have always had about such things. So I put an ache in the heart of the law-gatherers, so that they might help with gathering in the pieces. It took four years, but they have gathered many pieces – enough – I think – for us to get started. They even made some frames for us to use for our work if we want. It will be hard work," said the grandmother, "but at least we will be together doing it, and, who knows, maybe others will start to join us."

The girls looked at each other, and that is when they realized that four years had gone by, rather than four days. Even Sky said nothing now. Their grandmother had paused to let that sink in, but now she continued. "It is like making a hide." The girls looked at each other again. They had both helped their parents with hides, and knew it was the hardest physical work they had ever done. And there were all the steps, all the little things you had to know, the skills you had to learn by doing them, often by doing them wrong at that. "It's like making a hide," their grandmother repeated. "And just like when you finish one hide, another one is waiting to be made. Every generation," she told them, "is responsible for making and remaking our laws. It is hard work, and work that is never complete. This is what I have brought to you, if you want it."

The girls were silent, letting this all soak in. They eyed the frames the law-gatherers had made, which indeed looked like the four poles tied together with sinew that you lace the hide onto for scraping it. And even this took work, making sure the frame fit, and changing it as necessary, pausing to tighten the laces as they got looser as you scraped. If the law was like a hide, and one that you never finished making, they were not so sure the grandmother had brought them a gift. "Of course," she added, smiling, "just like making a hide, you need to take breaks too." Sky smiled. She was good at taking breaks. So good, in fact, she often got in trouble at school for this very thing. Something in this project appealed to her sense of adventure and desire to create. She was sure she could feel the strength of her ancestors beating in her veins as she gazed at the marvellous scene in front of them. But Claire was troubled and unsure about the gift. Didn't law need something more than just two young girls and a grandmother in a dream? If they started, would more people come? Would it make a difference at all? So much had already been tried. So much had failed to stem the rushing, roaring, flow of pain. People were weary and wary of yet another "solution." Everyone was so busy just trying to survive these days, how to ask people to take on yet another task, for such an uncertain outcome.

As if their grandmother had heard her thoughts, she put a gentle hand on Claire's shoulder. "Whatever you do," she said, "you will not be alone." Then she put another hand on Sky's. "It will not be easy. Sometimes you will be so tired you will cry, and sometimes you will be so sad you'll want to sleep forever. And whatever you do, you will have to stand up for each other, and for other children yet to come. No matter what, you will still have to find the strength within to do this, again and again, for yourselves, for the children yet to come, and for the generations after you." She took both girls' hands in hers. "A long time ago, and even sometimes today, these laws gave people something to lean on, and the strength to stand together against fear and horror. It is my gift, to you, gathered by law-gatherers. It is here, for you and the generations after you, from generations before you. It is ours. It is yours if you want it."

The two girls and the grandmother stood hand-in-hand by the river, thinking about all these things, and for a moment, all three could feel, in the distance, the brightness coming back to them.

Bibliography

Books and Articles

Abell, Jennie, and Elizabeth Sheehy. *Criminal Law and Procedure: Cases, Context and Critique*. 3rd ed. Concord, ON: Captus, 2002.

Adjin-Tettey, Elizabeth. "Sentencing Aboriginal Offenders: Balancing Offenders' Needs, the Interests of Victims and Society, and the Process of Decolonization of Aboriginal Peoples." *Canadian Journal of Women and the Law* 19 (2007): 179–216.

Amnesty International. *Stolen Sisters: A Human Rights Approach to Discrimination and Violence against Indigenous Women in Canada*. 2004. https://www.amnesty.ca/sites/amnesty/files/amr200032004enstolensisters.pdf.

Arendt, Hannah. *Eichmann in Jerusalem: A Report on the Banality of Evil*. London: Faber and Faber, 1963.

– *The Human Condition*. Chicago: University of Chicago Press, 1958.

Bartlett, Katharine T. "Tradition, Change, and the Idea of Progress in Feminist Legal Thought." *Wisconsin Law Review* 1 (1995): 303–43.

Bauman, Carol-Ann. "The Sentencing of Sexual Offences against Children." *Criminal Reports* 17 (1998): 352–66.

Beckett, Katherine. "Culture and the Politics of Signification: The Case of Child Sexual Abuse." *Social Problems* 43, no. 1 (1996): 57–76.

Borrows, John. *Canada's Indigenous Constitution*. Toronto: University of Toronto Press, 2010.

– "Crown and Aboriginal Occupations of Land: A History & Comparison." Research paper prepared for the Ipperwash Inquiry (2005). https://www.attorneygeneral.jus.gov.on.ca/inquiries/ipperwash/policy_part/research/pdf/History_of_Occupations_Borrows.pdf.

- "Physical Philosophy: Mobility and the Future of Indigenous Rights."
  In *Indigenous Peoples and the Law: Comparative and Critical Perspectives*, ed.
  Benjamin J. Richardson, Shin Imai, and Kent McNeil, 403–20. Portland, OR:
  Hart Publishing, 2009.
- *Recovering Canada: The Resurgence of Indigenous Law*. Toronto: University of
  Toronto Press, 2006.
- "With or Without You: First Nations Law in Canada." *McGill Law Journal* 41
  (1996): 629–65.

Borrows, John, Maureen Maloney, and Dawnis Kennedy. *An Assessment of the
Interrelationship between Economic and Justice Strategies in Urban Aboriginal
Communities*. Vol. 1. Victoria, BC: University of Victoria, Institute for Dispute
Resolution and Faculty of Law, 2005.

Borrows, John, and Leonard Rotman. *Aboriginal Legal Issues: Cases, Materials,
and Commentary*. 2nd ed. Toronto: LexisNexis Canada, 2003.

Boyden, Joseph. *Three Day Road*. Toronto: Penguin Books, 2005.

Brightman, Robert. "The Windigo in the Material World." *Ethnohistory* 35,
no. 4 (1988): 337–79.

Brightman, Robert, David Meyer, and Lou Marano. "On Windigo Psychosis."
Current Anthropology 21, no. 1 (1983): 120–5.

Brown, Jennifer S.H., and Robert Brightman. *The Orders of the Dreamed: George
Nelson on Cree and Northern Ojibwa Religion and Myth, 1923*. Winnipeg:
University of Manitoba Press, 1990.

Brunnée, Jutta, and Stephen Toope. "An Interactional Theory of International
Legal Obligation." University of Toronto Faculty of Law, Legal Research
Series no. 08-16, 2008. https://papers.ssrn.com/sol3/papers.cfm?abstract_
id=1162882.

Carlson, Nathan D. "Appendix Cases." In "Reviving the Wihtikow: Cannibal
Monsters in Northern Alberta Cree and Metis Cosmology." BA thesis,
University of Alberta, 2005.

- "Reviving Witiko (Windigo): An Ethnohistory of 'Cannibal Monsters' in the
  Athabasca District of Northern Alberta, 1878–1910." *Ethnohistory* 56, no. 3
  (2009): 355–94.

Clemmons, John C., Kate Walsh, David DiLillo, and Terri L. Messman-Moore.
"Unique and Combined Contributions of Multiple Child Abuse Types and
Abuse Severity to Adult Trauma Symptomatology." *Child Maltreatment* 12,
no. 2 (2007): 172–81.

Coulthard, Glen S. "Subjects of the Empire: Indigenous Peoples and the 'Politics
of Recognition' in Canada." *Contemporary Political Theory* 6 (2007): 437–60.

DeCoste, F.C. Review of *Law after Auschwitz*, by David Fraser. *Kings Law
Journal* 18 (2007): 179–87.

Fiddler, Thomas, and James R. Stevens. *Killing the Shaman*. Newcastle, ON: Penumbra, 1991.

Finkelhor, David. *Childhood Victimization: Violence, Crime and Abuse in the Lives of Young People*. New York: Oxford University Press, 2008.

Finkelhor, David, and Associates. *A Sourcebook on Child Sexual Abuse*. Beverly Hills, CA: Sage Publications, 1986.

Fogelson, Raymond D. "Windigo Goes South: Stoneclad among the Cherokees." In *Manlike Monsters on Trial: Early Records and Modern Evidence*, ed. Marjorie Halpin and Michael M. Ames, 132–50. Vancouver: UBC Press, 1980.

Forbes, Jack D. *Columbus and Other Cannibals: The Wetiko Disease of Exploitation, Imperialism and Terrorism*. Rev. ed. Toronto: Seven Stories, 2008.

Fuller, Lon L. *The Morality of Law*. New Haven, CT: Yale University Press, 1964.

Gerring, John. *Social Sciences Methodology: A Criterial Framework*. New York: Cambridge University Press, 2001.

Glenn, H. Patrick. "The Capture, Reconstruction and Marginalization of 'Custom.'" *American Journal of Comparative Law* 45, no. 3 (1997): 613–20.

Greenspan, Edward L., and Marc Rosenberg. *Martin's Annual Criminal Code 2006*. Aurora, ON: Canada Law Book, 2006.

Harring, Sidney L. "The Enforcement of the Extreme Penalty: Canadian Law and the Ojibwa-Cree Spirit World." In *White Man's Law: Native People in Nineteenth-Century Canadian Jurisprudence*, ed. Sidney L. Harring, 217–38. Toronto: University of Toronto Press, 1998.

Hart, H.L.A. *The Concept of Law*. 2nd ed. New York: Oxford University Press, 1994.

Haugaard, Jeffrey J., and Cindy Hazan. "Recognizing and Treating Uncommon Behavioral and Emotional Disorders in Children and Adolescents Who Have Been Severely Maltreated: Reactive Attachment Disorder." *Child Maltreatment* 9 (2004): 154–60.

Herman, Judith. *Trauma and Recovery: The Aftermath of Violence; From Domestic Violence to Political Terror*. New York: Basic Books, 1997.

Hylton, John H. *Aboriginal Sexual Offending in Canada*. 2nd ed. Ottawa: Ontario Aboriginal Healing Foundation, 2006. http://www.ahf.ca/downloads/revisedsexualoffending_reprint.pdf.

Johnston, Basil. *The Manitous: The Supernatural World of the Ojibway*. Toronto: Key Porter Books, 1995.

Kagan, Richard, and Shirley Schlosberg. *Families in Perpetual Crisis*. Markham, ON: Penguin Books, 1989.

Kline, Marlee. "Child Welfare Law, 'Best Interests of the Child' Ideology, and First Nations." *Osgoode Hall Law Journal* 30 (1992): 375–425.

Krygier, Martin. "Law as Tradition." *Law and Philosophy* 5, no. 2 (1986): 237–62.

LaRocque, Emma. "Re-examining Culturally Appropriate Models of Criminal Justice." In *Aboriginal and Treaty Rights in Canada*, ed. Michael Asch, 75–96. Vancouver: UBC Press, 1997.

Law Commission of Canada. *Justice Within: Indigenous Legal Traditions*. DVD. Ottawa: Minister of Supply and Services Canada, 2006.

MacMartin, Clare, and Linda A. Wood. "Sexual Motives and Sentencing: Judicial Discourse in Cases of Child Sexual Abuse." *Journal of Language and Social Psychology* 24, no. 2 (2005): 139–59.

MacDonald, Roderick A., and Jason MacLean. "Navigating the Transsystemic: No Toilets in the Park." *McGill Law Journal* 50 (2005): 721–87.

Marano, Lou, Charles Bishop, M. Jean Black, William M. Bolman, Jennifer Brown, Thomas H. Hay, Marshall G. Hurlich, Ruth Landes, H.F. McGee, H.B.M. Murphy, J. Anthony Paredes, Richard Preston, Robin Ridington, Vivian Rohrl, James G.E. Smith, R.J. Smith, Morton Teicher, David Turner, Leo Waisberg, and Hazel H. Weidman. "Windigo Psychosis: The Anatomy of an Emic-Etic Confusion [and Comments and Reply]." *Current Anthropology* 23, no. 4 (1982): 385–412.

McGillivray, Anne, and Brenda Comaskey. *Black Eyes All of the Time: Intimate Violence, Aboriginal Women, and the Justice System*. Toronto: University of Toronto Press, 1999.

McLeod, Neal. *Cree Narrative Memory: From Treaties to Contemporary Times*. Saskatoon: Purich Publishing, 2007.

Napoleon, Val. "Ayook: Gitksan Legal Order, Law, and Legal Theory." PhD diss., University of Victoria Faculty of Law, 2009.

Napoleon, Val, Angela Cameron, Colette Arcand, and Dahti Scott. "Where's the Law in Restorative Justice?" In *Aboriginal Self-Government in Canada: Current Trends and Issues*, 3rd ed. Saskatoon: Purich Publishing, 2008.

Norman, Howard. *Where the Chill Came From: Cree Windigo Tales and Journeys*. San Francisco: North Point, 1982.

Perry, Garry P., and Janet Orchard. *Assessment and Treatment of Adolescent Sex Offenders*. Sarasota, FL: Professional Resource, 1992.

Podruchny, Carolyn. "Werewolves and Windigos: Narratives of Cannibal Monsters in French-Canadian Voyageur Tradition." *Ethnohistory* 5, no. 4 (2004): 677–700.

Postema, Gerald. "Classical Common Law Jurisprudence, Part II." *Oxford Commonwealth Law Journal* 3 (2003): 1–28.

Preston, Richard J. "The Witiko: Algonkian Knowledge and Whiteman Knowledge." In *Manlike Monsters on Trial: Early Records and Modern Evidence*, ed. Marjorie Halpin and Michael M. Ames, 111–31. Vancouver: UBC Press, 1980.

Raz, Joseph. "Can There Be a Theory of Law?" In *The Blackwell Guide to the Philosophy of Law and Legal Theory*, ed. Martin P. Golding and William A. Edmundson, 324–51. Oxford: Blackwell Publishing, 2005.

Ridington, Robin. "Wechuge and Windigo: A Comparison of Cannibal Belief among Boreal Forest Athapaskans and Algonquians." In *Little Bit Know Something: Stories in the Language of Anthropology*, 107–29. Vancouver: Douglas and McIntyre, 1990.

Ross, Rupert. *Returning to the Teachings: Exploring Aboriginal Justice*. Toronto: Penguin Books, 1996.

– "Traumatization in Remote First Nations: An Expression of Concern." 2006. Author's collection.

Rundle, Kristen. "The Impossibility of an Exterminatory Legality: Law and the Holocaust." *University of Toronto Law Journal* 59 (2009): 486–504.

Santos, Boaventura de Sousa. "A Critique of Lazy Reason: Against the Waste of Experience." Paper presented to the DemCon Conference, 1 December 2006.

– *The World Social Forum: A User's Manual*. Coimbra: Centre for Social Studies, 2004. http://www.ces.uc.pt/bss/documentos/fsm_eng.pdf.

Savage, Candice, ed. *The World of Wetiko: Tales from the Woodland Cree, as Told by Marie Merasty*. Saskatoon, SK: Saskatchewan Indian Cultural College, 1974.

Scott, Sheryn T. "Multiple Traumatic Experiences and the Development of Posttraumatic Stress Disorder." *Journal of Interpersonal Violence* 22, no. 7 (2007): 932–8.

Stavast, Kendall. "Cosmology, Self and Legal Order in Subarctic Athapaskan Society." 2008. Author's collection.

Stewart, Wendy, Audrey Huntley, and Fay Blaney. *The Implications of Restorative Justice for Aboriginal Women and Children Survivors of Violence: A Comparative Overview of Five Communities in British Columbia*. Ottawa: Law Commission of Canada, 2001.

Teicher, Morton. "Windigo Psychosis: A Study of a Relationship between Belief and Behavior among the Indians of Northeastern Canada." In *Proceedings of the 1960 Annual Spring Meeting of the American Ethnological Society*, ed. Verne F. Ray, 1–129. Seattle: University of Washington Press, 1960.

Tully, James. "Two Meanings of Global Citizenship: Modern and Diverse." Paper presented to the Meanings of Global Citizenship Conference, 9–10 September 2005. http://webcache.googleusercontent.com/search?q=cache:R4YtQgWaQS0J:www.law.uvic.ca/demcon/documents/Tully%2520Presem%2520-%2520Two%2520Meanings%2520of%2520Global%2520Citizenship%2520II.doc+&cd=1&hl=en&ct=clnk&gl=ca.

Turpel-Lafond, Mary Ellen. "Some Thoughts on Inclusion and Innovation in the Saskatchewan Justice System." *Saskatchewan Law Review* 68 (2005): 293–302.

Waldram, James B. *Revenge of the Windigo: The Construction of the Mind and Mental Health of North American Aboriginal Peoples.* Toronto: University of Toronto Press, 2004.

Webber, Jeremy. "The Grammar of Customary Law." *McGill Law Journal* 54, no. 4 (2009): 579–626.

Weber, Gregory M. "Grooming Children for Sexual Abuse." TULIR, Centre for the Prevention and Healing of Child Sexual Abuse, 2010. http://www.tulir.org/grooming.htm.

Widdowson, Frances, and Albert Howard. *Disrobing the Aboriginal Industry: The Deception behind Indigenous Cultural Preservation.* Montreal and Kingston: McGill-Queen's University Press, 2008.

Wild, Rex, and Patricia Anderson. *Ampe Akelyernemane Meke Mekarle, "Little Children Are Sacred": Report of the Northern Territory Board of Inquiry into the Protection of Aboriginal Children from Sexual Abuse.* Darwin, AU: Northern Territory Government, 2007.

Interviews

Interview #1: Interview of elders Adelaide McDonald and Norman McDonald, 11 April 2009, Alberta.

Interview #2: Interview of anonymous elder, 13 April 2009, Alberta.

Interview #3: Interview of anonymous community member, 13 April 2009, Alberta.

Interview #4: Interview of anonymous community leader, 13 June 2009, Alberta.

Interview #5: Interview of two anonymous young adult community members, 14 June 2009, Alberta.

Interview #6: Interview of anonymous community member, 14 June 2009, Alberta.

Cases

R v Machekequonabe [1897] OJ No 98, 2 CCC 138.

R v Michel and Cecil Courtreille, PAA Acc: 79.266/126 Box 1. Edmonton Supreme Court Files.

Legislation

Criminal Code, RSC 1985, c C-46.

Online Resources

Aboriginal Healing Foundation. http://www.ahf.ca/about-us/mission.
Caruso, Kevin. "Suicide by Cop." Suicide.org. http://www.suicide.org/
suicide-by-cop.html.
Correctional Services of Canada. "Let's Talk." http://www.csc-scc.gc.ca/text/
pblct/lt-en/2006/31-3/7-eng.shtml.
Little Warriors. http://www.littlewarriors.ca.
"Schedule 'N,' Mandate for the Truth and Reconciliation Commission."
http://www.residentialschoolsettlement.ca/SCHEDULE_N.pdf.
TULIR, Centre for the Prevention & Healing of Child Sexual Abuse. http://
www.tulir.org/grooming.htm.

Newspaper Articles

McClearn, Matthew, and Kathryn Blaze Baum. "The Taken: Who Qualifies
as a Serial Killer and More on Data behind the Project." *Globe and Mail*,
23 November 2015. https://beta.theglobeandmail.com/news/national/
the-taken-who-qualifies-as-a-serial-killer-and-more-on-the-data-behind-the-
project/article27443307/?ref=http://www.theglobeandmail.com&.
National Post. "The Verdict on Sentencing Circles," 18 February 2009. http://
www.pressreader.com/canada/national-post-latest-edition/20090218/
281822869698430.
Simon, Paula. "Relatives Not Automatically Best Caregivers for Child in
Need." *Edmonton Journal*, 31 January 2009.